RELIGION AND THE
PRESIDENTIAL ELECTION

Copublished with the Eagleton Institute of Politics,
Rutgers University

RELIGION AND THE PRESIDENTIAL ELECTION

Paul Lopatto

American Political Parties and Elections

general editor:
Gerald M. Pomper

PRAEGER SPECIAL STUDIES • PRAEGER SCIENTIFIC

New York • Philadelphia • Eastbourne, UK
Toronto • Hong Kong • Tokyo • Sydney

Library of Congress Cataloging in Publication Data

Lopatto, Paul.
    Religion and the presidential election.

    Bibliography: p.
    Includes index.
    1. Presidents--United States--Election. 2. Voting--
United States. 3. United States--Politics and govern-
ment--1945--   . 4. Religion and politics--United
States. I. Title.
JK524.L67 1985   324.973   84-26281
ISBN 0-03-001474-3 (alk. paper)

36.95

9-17-90

Published in 1985 by Praeger Publishers
CBS Educational and Professional Publishing
a Division of CBS Inc.
521 Fifth Avenue, New York, NY 10175 USA

© 1985 by Praeger Publishers

56789 052 987654321

Printed in the United States of America
on acid-free paper

To Paul Allen Beck

Preface

The results of all research projects must ultimately be judged against the goals of those who undertake them. Thus from the perspective of the reader, it is best that these goals be laid out as early as possible.

When this project was conceived, there seemed to be very little interest among students of American elections in determining the exact role that religious values and beliefs play in the political system. While distinctions were commonly made between Catholic and Protestant voters, only a few researchers such as Kathy Frankovic and Albert Menendez sought to undertake more serious studies of the effect of religion on electoral behavior. Though the reason for this lack of interest is not perfectly clear, there seemed to be a common assumption among political scientists that religion was no longer an important enough variable to merit serious study. The 1980 election changed all that. In that year strenuous organizing efforts on the part of certain groups on the religious right began to receive serious media attention. The surprisingly lopsided victory of Ronald Reagan and impressive Republican gains in congressional races opened the way for the leadership of the religious right to claim an important role in the election outcome.

Since these claims carried with them the possibility of vastly increased political influence on the part of right-wing religious groups, they could not be expected to go unchallenged. Before long the academic world began to respond. Numerous articles and papers devoted to the study of the new religious right have begun to appear. They have attempted to delineate such qualities of this group as its size, potential mass base of support, and ideological homogeniety. What seems to be lacking in these efforts is a sense of how this new right activity fits into the larger picture of religious influence in the American political system. This book results from an effort to provide just such an overall picture. Rather than focus on one specific religious group at one point in time we sought to examine each of the major Christian denominational groups over an extended series of presidential elections.

Our most basic goal is to establish religion as a major explanatory variable in the study of American presidential voting behavior. Presidential elections, of course, are not the only important electoral events in the American political universe. However, they are far and away the most visible episodes in the electoral cycle and, unlike more localized elections, they possess the capacity to set the tone for the entire political system. As such they represent the logical starting point for determining the exact role that religion plays in American politics.

The main focus of the study is the six most recent presidential elections, running from 1960 through 1980. These are the six years for which adequate survey data are available. The specific tasks include measuring the link between religion and presidential voting in each of these years and explaining exactly how this linkage takes place. The method of approach can best be understood by briefly outlining the goals of each chapter.

Chapter 1 is composed of two separate parts. The first attempts to summarize the history of the effect of religion on presidential voting behavior from the early years of the republic to the modern period. Aside from setting the context, this historical material is used to develop theoretical propositions that attempt to explain the rise and fall of the religion factor over time. These propositions are developed in the second part. Briefly stated, there are two separate components to this implicit model of change, one long-term and one short-term. The short-term factor is the nomination of the presidential candidates themselves. These candidates, through the issue stands they take and the personal images they present, can activate or suppress the effect of religion on the vote. This, of course, will vary from one election to the next. The long-term factor involves changes at the mass level. In particular, social, economic, and demographic changes can lead to changes in the relative status positions of the various religious groups. Those who feel their status to be declining are likely to be motivated to turn to government action as a way of halting these unfavorable trends. During such periods the basic religious cleavages inherent in American society will be intensified. This ultimately will be reflected in a heightened relationship between religion and voting behavior.

Chapter 2 examines the exact nature of these religious cleavages. It attempts to describe the conflicting religious perspectives held by Americans, perspectives that could potentially lead to political conflict. The analysis flows from the development of a denominational categorization scheme that is shown to be a meaningful predictor of three different types of religious belief.

Chapter 3 examines the actual relationship between religious belief, as measured by the denominational categorization scheme, and presidential voting behavior. It is shown that large differences exist among the denominational groups regarding their partisan voting decisions in a number of recent presidential elections. These voting differences remain, even when controls for other social variables are applied.

The findings of Chapter 3 offer strong evidence that a key explanation for the rise and fall in the influence of the religion factor on the vote is the nature of the presidential candidates themselves. This proposition is tested more directly in Chapter 4 through the use of simulated election analysis. It is shown that, even when time is held constant, different individuals hold very different appeals for the respective religious groups. In addition, the data complement Chapter 3 by offering further evidence for the existence of strong and politically relevant religious cleavages in the American electorate.

Chapter 5 attempts to explain exactly how these religious cleavages come to affect the vote. The ways that religious beliefs are related to various types of political issues are examined.

Chapter 6 moves to examine the more long-term factor affecting the relationship between religion and the vote. It attempts to uncover changes at the mass level that could account for an upswing in the intensity of religious-political conflict in recent years. Specifically, we will look for possible sources of feelings of status decline that could be motivating the modern religious right to increase their efforts to use political action to achieve religious ends.

Finally, Chapter 7 attempts to examine the possibility that religious beliefs may be affecting the formation of partisan identification among many younger voters. The importance of such an examination stems from the possible long-term implications of this sort of partisan change. This topic leads us inevitably to speculate about the future course of American electoral politics. The wisdom contained in this final section will then await verification by the political events of the years to come.

Acknowledgments

In the course of undertaking this research project I have come to understand that no scholarly work is ever entirely the product of the author's own efforts. Along the way there have been numerous influences on my thinking. Aside from the scholars whose works I have cited in the text, I owe a strong debt to a few individuals with whom I have had much more direct contact. I am grateful to Jim Stimson, Jim Fendrich, and Scott Flanagan for their helpful comments and criticisms, which were of great use in the development of both theory and methodology. I also wish to thank Dorothy Davidson, Steve Renten, and Yvette Nowak for their ideas and technical help, which proved invaluable at many points along the way. But my biggest debt is owed to Paul Allen Beck, whose patient guidance over the years has made possible whatever contributions I am able to make to the fields of social research and professional scholarship.

Contents

History and Change

INTRODUCTION

All who attempt to explain human conflict must inevitably become students of history. Whether we speak of sibling rivalries or world wars, the ultimate origins of conflict are to be found somewhere in the past. Thus our attempt to explain the religious element in recent political conflict must begin with an acknowledgment of what has gone before.

For this reason it seems wise to begin with a brief overview of the role played by religion in American presidential politics in the years prior to the advent of extensive survey research in the 1950s. Among other things, the first section will make it clear that the importance of this role has varied greatly over time, rising in some periods and falling in others.

The second section will attempt to address directly this question of change. We will draw upon the historical material to develop a set of theoretical propositions to explain this pattern of change in the relationship between religion and voting behavior over time. In later chapters we will make use of these theoretical notions as we seek to achieve our ultimate goal of explaining religious influence in more recent presidential elections.

RELIGION IN AMERICAN POLITICAL HISTORY

The First Party System

The influence of religion on American voting behavior can be seen as early as the formation of the first party system in the first decade following the ratification of the Constitution. "The Episcopalian and Congregationalist churches became identified with the conservative Federalists and Whigs, while the Baptist, Methodist, and Presbyterian churches were linked with the Jeffersonians and Jacksonians."[1] In terms of empirical historical analysis, this religious cleavage is somewhat difficult to separate from the other major cleavage on which the first party system was built, that of class. This difficulty stems from the fact that the Episcopalian and Congregationalist churches attracted adherents disproportionately from the upper classes in their respective areas of the country, the Congregationalists in the North and the Episcopalians in the South.[2]

Nevertheless, there is convincing evidence that religion did become an independent political force in its own right during this early period. Perhaps more than anything else, this religious cleavage centered around the question of whether or not the various states should be allowed to designate particular denominations as official state churches. Although the Bill of Rights prohibited Congress from recognizing an official national church, it was not until the passage of the Fourteenth Amendment in 1866 that this provision was extended to the states. As a consequence, many state legislatures did in fact proclaim the politically dominant denomination to be their official state church. In the North, this meant that the Congregationalists tended to gain official state recognition. In the South, the Episcopalians were generally able to attain this same honor.[3]

Because it was the Federalists who attempted to secure this legal advantage for the Congregationalists and Episcopalians, the losing Protestant denominations were forced to seek an alliance with the opposition Jeffersonian Democrats. This helps to explain a seeming paradox inherent in this set of political alliances. As Lipset points out, the leaders of the Democratic-Republican party tended to be the secularists of their day. "They tended to look upon much of organized religion and most of the theologies of their day as outmoded medieval beliefs which would dwindle away."[4] The Federalist leadership, on the other hand, tended to be more traditional in its religious outlook. At first glance, one would tend to think that the highly moralistic and religiously orthodox lower Protestant groups would have found more in common with the Federalists than with their more secular foes. However, when we recognize the intensity of the battle over disestablishment, more sense can be made of the situation. The Baptists, Methodists, and Presbyterians of this period were reacting against this Federalist attempt to make them second-class citizens in their own country. Religion, then, tended to affect political behavior through the old-fashioned mechanism of group self-interest.[5]

Nonetheless, it would be a mistake to assume that the religion factor operated only through this concern with group self-preservation. A second way that religion can become politically relevant is by bringing to the forefront questions of public morality and its inevitable tendency to conflict with personal liberty. While the importance of denominational conflict over disestablishment should not be understated, there is evidence that a second religious cleavage, one based more purely on moral issues, was also influencing the politics of the time. The libertarian views of the Democratic leadership did not sit well with the Federalists, many of whom were Congregationalist clergymen. "They argued that the state was a proper instrument to eradicate moral evils such as gambling and 'grog selling,' while the Democrats sought to limit the role of the state to the prevention of evils which resulted from individuals or groups being interfered with by others."[6]

It is this second form of religious conflict that is of greater concern to our study. By 1833 all of the states had officially disestablished their state churches, and this issue was forever banished from the American political agenda. Yet the conflict over the question of the relationship between church and state in the area of public morality was to reappear in many different forms throughout the next century and a half of the nation's history.

The Pre-Civil War Years

The religiously motivated concern over public morality was to play a major role in the nation's politics in the years preceding the Civil War. Most importantly, it was to play a major role in the partisan realignment of the more evangelistic Protestant groups, which had been largely completed by the outbreak of the war in 1861.

As stated earlier, the alliance of the Baptist, Methodist, and Presbyterian denominations with the Democratic party during the Jeffersonian and early Jacksonian periods had been based on a marriage of convenience between the secularist Democratic leadership and these lower-status Protestant groups who were opposed to the official state recognition of the higher-status churches. As this conflict over disestablishment subsided, the underpinnings for the alliance began to crumble. In addition, the rapid social, economic, and demographic changes of the first half of the nineteenth century brought about a substantial improvement in the relative status positions of the major evangelical Protestant groups. Economic growth allowed an increasing proportion of Baptists, Methodists, and Presbyterians to move into the middle class. Numerically, these groups also gained in strength due to the successful use of revivalism to win converts. By 1850, two-thirds of American Protestants were either Baptist or Methodist.[7]

During the first party system, concern with the domination of the high-status Protestant churches had forced the more evangelical groups to align themselves with the civil libertarians and to resist the temptation to use the power of the state to help bring into being their vision of a higher moral order.

> With the increase in numbers and influence of these ascendant Protestant groups went a corresponding increase in willingness to use state power to enforce "their morality." There was still a kind of parallel between the fight against the political establishment and the fight against the (now unofficial) religious establishment, but the Baptists and Methodists began to move to the "other side" of the fight. They joined the older-established Protestant churches and the prevailing conservative political party in raising moral concerns as public issues. A purely religious dimension entered as a differentiating factor here.[8]

This gradual movement of the evangelical Protestant groups into the Whig and, later, the Republican ranks, was given impetus by the arrival of waves of Catholic immigrants who generally found a political home in the Democratic party. These Catholic immigrants brought with them a set of social norms, such as relatively liberal views on the use of alcohol, which were often at odds with the strongly held moral beliefs of the evangelicals.

The politicized religious conflict of these pre-Civil War decades took a number of specific forms. Adding to this complexity was the existence of a number of important third-party movements that took on a strongly religious tone. One issue that divided the various religious groups was that of temperance. The concern of many Federalist and Whig leaders with the social problems caused by drinking had a natural appeal for many evangelicals. As the issue of disestablishment declined and the status conflicts among Protestant denominations subsided, many evangelical leaders moved into the Whig party and took up the temperance cause. "As a matter of fact, the Baptists and Methodists called for more drastic measures than did the earlier temperance leaders. The former favored total abstinence and eventually the passage of prohibition legislation, whereas the latter had advocated education to secure moderate drinking."[9] When the Whig party collapsed, due largely to the slave issue, many of these same people moved into the new Republican party, causing the GOP to take on a protemperance slant.

A second issue that became of great importance, beginning in the 1830s, was that of abolition. Gradually, many of the evangelical Protestant clergy in the North began to define slavery as the greatest immorality of its time. This religious fervor added great impetus to the abolitionist movement in many Northern states. On the other hand, the Southern clergy of these same denominations used religious arguments to defend the institution of slavery and Southern culture in general against what they claimed to be blasphemous attacks from their Yankee counterparts. The result was the division of the Baptist, Methodist, and Presbyterian denominations into Northern and Southern wings. Members of the Northern wings tended to move into the newly emerging Republican party, because of its relatively clear stand on the slave issue. In response to this and to the Civil War itself, the membership of the Southern wings became all the more firmly attached to the Democratic party.[10]

Finally it should be mentioned that, in this period, the rise of American Catholicism was beginning to become an issue in itself. Significant third-party movements, such as the Anti-Masonic party in the 1830s and the Know-Nothings in the 1850s, were based largely on nativist anti-Catholic themes. In part, this nativism reflected the economic threat that the new waves of cheap labor from Europe provided to the Protestant working classes. Yet there was a distinctly religious anti-Catholic theme as well. "In addition, strong anti-papist sentiments still existed among various Protestant denominations. . . . Some religious conservatives, fearing a growing threat to their way of life in Catholic immigration, began to see signs of a plot by the hated Papists, by the Jesuit order."[11] These anti-Catholic third parties often served as way stations for evangelical Protestants on their way to the Whig or Republican parties.

By the start of the Civil War, the great partisan realignment of American religious groups had come to virtual completion. Most of the evangelical Protestant groups in the North had joined the upper-status Protestants in the new conservative party, the Republican party. On the other hand, each new wave of Catholic immigrants from Europe generally swelled the ranks of the Democracy. There they were joined by the remnants of the Southern wings of the evangelical denominations. This strange combination was to put a strain on national Democratic party strategists for the next century.

The Post-Civil War Years

The years following the end of the Civil War saw the emergence of a period of relative stability in the partisan alignments of the major American religious groups. This period began with the almost complete domination of national politics by the Republican party. Gradually, however, the Democratic party gained in strength and, by the 1880s, the two major parties had reached a point of virtual electoral equality at the national level. In part, this evening-out of the parties simply reflected the readmission of the Democratic-dominated Southern states into the union. "But, it also reflected decline in Republican strength in those regions where the party had been strongest in 1860."[12]

Paul Kleppner's major study of Midwestern politics in the second half of the nineteenth century provides strong evidence that, at least in the Midwest, this Republican decline was intimately connected with the basic partisan religious cleavage. Kleppner characterized the struggle as one that pitted pietistic religious groups against those with a more liturgical orientation. Pietists tended to dominate those Protestant denominations that we have previously referred to as evangelistic in outlook. They tended to place emphasis on right behavior and on taking actions to rid the world of sin and establish a higher moral order. The liturgicals were dominant among Catholics and certain German Lutheran groups that had remained close to the Catholic tradition. The liturgicals emphasized right doctrine and generally rejected the idea that the world could be made more moral through the forced application of strict social norms.[13] The major political battles between these two distinct religious tendencies usually concerned prohibition and control of parochial and public school systems. The latter issue took on particular intensity, for it meant control of the mechanisms through which new generations could be socialized into one orientation or the other.

When the pietists went on the political attack, it was usually through the vehicle of the Republican party. Not surprisingly, this forced their liturgical opponents into the Democratic ranks. The resulting alignment created strategic problems for the Republicans, which largely accounted for their gradual decline. For one thing, most new immigrants were liturgicals. Therefore, as long as the religious cleavage remained the chief underpinning of the party system, the Republicans were bound to lose strength. One possible solution was to attempt to deemphasize this religious cleavage and replace it with a different one. However, attempts by Republican strategists to accomplish this often resulted in the alienation of many pietists and their withdrawal into more purist third parties such as the Prohibitionists.[14]

This general dilemma, faced by Republican party leaders in the years before 1896, is also documented in the work of Richard Jensen. Adherence by the Republican leadership to basic pietistic principles brought them temporary victories in a number of Midwestern states. However, the backlash effects of pietistic policies brought inevitable electoral defeat, leaving these political elites in a position of having to purge radical pietists from the party and start rebuilding all over again.[15]

The events of 1896 finally provided Republican strategists with the opportunity to break out of this dilemma. Partly as a result of the chaos brought about by the depression of 1893, a new group of leaders was able to seize control of the national Democratic party. The campaign of the fundamentalist, William Jennings Bryan, with its evangelistic style and its attempt to treat politics as a moral crusade, was well received by many pietists who had previously seen the Democratic party as the great enemy. On the other hand, the strategy of the national Republican party, led by William McKinley, was to expand the social base of the party by playing down divisive cultural issues and emphasizing the need to return to economic prosperity. The net effect of the two strategies was to bring about a temporary realignment in some parts of the country, with many pietists supporting Bryan while their liturgical opponents moved over to vote for McKinley.[16]

The Twentieth Century

In spite of its substantial short-term effects, the election of 1896 can best be viewed as a temporary interruption in the basic partisan religious cleavage that had been solidified by the time of the Civil War. As Lipset suggests, "the rural Midwestern votes which Bryan brought to the Democrats from the Populists in 1896 and 1900 returned to the Republican fold with the candidacy of Theodore Roosevelt in 1904."[17] A similar conclusion is reached by James Sundquist in his important study of party alignments in American history.[18]

The next significant interruption in the basic correlation between religion and partisan voting occurred in 1920. In this case, however, the deviation from the normal pattern was a result of the intervention of a second factor, ethnicity, which correlated highly with religious preference. The failure of the Wilson administration to keep America out of World War I resulted in an anti-Democratic reaction on the part of the largely Catholic Germans and Irish in the first presidential election following that war. These defections largely continued in 1924, as many members of the alienated ethnic groups chose to cast their votes for the Progressive candidate, Robert LaFollette.[19]

Also of significance in the 1920s was the rise of the Ku Klux Klan to a membership of between 3 and 6 million and a position of great political influence in many states. Central to the ideology of the Klan was a traditional Protestant moralism.[20] In fact, the prominent role played by the Klan in the Republican party probably helped to prevent the latter from solidifying the support of the disaffected Catholics.[21]

The nomination by the Democrats of the first Catholic presidential candidate of a major party in 1928 finally put an end to this latest deviation from the basic partisan religious alignment. "The election of 1928 played a major role in structuring the subsequent alignment of American voters. It clearly brought back to the national Democratic party all of the immigrant Catholic and Jewish vote which it had lost after World War I — and even added some."[22] Although Roosevelt was able to make substantial gains among many population groups, the basic correlation between religious preference and partisan vote was not significantly altered. Consequently, as of the 1950s, religious preference ranked along with social class as the major social cleavages on which the American party system was built.[23]

EXPLAINING CHANGE

Even this brief summary of the influence of religion on voting behavior in American history makes it clear that the strength of the religion factor has varied over time. For instance, religious values seemed to play a major role in the third-party movements of the Jacksonian era and in the rise of abolitionist sentiment just prior to the Civil War. In the postwar era, the outcomes of the tightly contested partisan battles in the Midwest depended greatly on the rise and fall of divisive religious issues from one election to the next. The presidential elections of 1896 and 1928 saw important religious groups line up differentially behind one or the other of the major candidates, although the religious alignments produced by the former election varied substantially from those produced by the latter. Finally, the 1920s witnessed the emergence of a fundamentalist Protestant backlash expressed, in part, through the rise of the Ku Klux Klan.

This section of the chapter will attempt to address the question of why the influence of religion on voting behavior seems to vary over time. Specifically, a set of theoretical propositions concerning change will be introduced. The first of these deals with the influence of political elites on the religion factor. The second concerns various forms of status displacement and their effect on the politicalization of mass religious movements. Finally, some attention will be paid to the development and nature of evangelical Protestantism and its important role in American religious-political movements.

The goal of this section is the development of theoretical propositions that can be stated in testable form. Since our ultimate goal is the explanation of contemporary political events, these will then be applied to the modern survey period and tested in later chapters.

Religion and Changes at the Elite Level

Proposition: All other things being equal, the influence of religion on voting behavior in presidential elections will be positively related to the tendency of the major candidates to give off politically relevant religious cues.

This proposition may seem, at first, to be merely a statement of the obvious. Potential voters react to the cues that the candidates offer them. However, it is important to distinguish conceptually between two different kinds of electoral change. In the first kind, changes at the elite level lead to changes at the level of mass voting behavior. New candidates and issues appear on the political horizon. Voters then respond to these changes in their political environment.

However, electoral change can also originate at the mass level and flow upward. Various kinds of economic, social, and demographic changes can result in the rise of mass social movements that can eventually work their way into the electoral system. In reality, this latter kind of change is not completely separable from the former. It is possible for mass social movements to lead to elite changes as candidates scramble to find issues that will strike positive chords in the mass electorate. Alternatively, the political issues that stem from social, economic, and demographic changes may remain latent until a colorful politician finds the right way to articulate them.

In spite of the close relationship between these two kinds of electoral change, there is value in keeping them conceptually distinct. In terms of the subject at hand, this distinction will allow us to be more precise when attempting to determine exactly how the influence of religion on voting behavior rises and falls with the passage of time. In this section we will concern ourselves with the influence that the presidential candidates, themselves, have on this sort of electoral change.

The presidential nominees of the major American political parties are in a position of extraordinary visibility in the months and weeks prior to the November election. Therefore, they are capable of giving off a whole host of cues that can rebound off the religious value systems of individual voters and alter their actual voting behavior. The kinds of cues that can be religiously and politically relevant are numerous. The candidates may take overt issue positions that for various reasons may have political relevance to this or that religious group. Examples of this in the past have included prohibitionism and abolitionism. Alternatively, presidential candidates, through the personal images they present, may give off cues relating to the nature of their personal value systems, quite apart from any policy proposals that they may articulate. These image cues can then be interpreted either positively or negatively by each of the nation's religious groups. Finally, the religious identification of the candidate can serve as a powerful cue through which voters can infer certain types of values and beliefs that they may or may not like in a potential president.

A few examples from the presurvey period of American history may serve to clarify things. Perhaps the most obvious example of presidential candidates affecting the relationship between religion and voting behavior occurred in the election of 1896. Historical analysis suggests that certain aspects of the candidacy of the Democratic nominee, William Jennings Bryan, temporarily increased the intensity of the partisan division between religious pietists and their more liturgical counterparts in a number of Midwestern states. The importance of the Bryan candidacy is attested to by the fact that it helped bring about a short-term change in the partisan allegiances of many voters. Many pietists, who usually felt much more at home in the Republican party, now found the Democratic nominee to be more in tune with their basic religious values than his largely secularist opponent. Not surprisingly, liturgical reaction to the same campaign often involved partisan movement in the opposite direction.[24]

Although Bryan had a reputation as a "dry," reaction to his campaign by the respective religious groups probably had less to do with any specific policy stands, which had direct religious significance, than from his campaign style and general philosophy of politics.

> Superficially, Bryan's speeches covered a multitude of topics — silver and gold, money and prices, banking, coercion, education, and the unrivalled beauty of the local countryside. At a deeper level, the level at which his audiences listened, his speeches were all the same, his words were all about good and evil, the righteous and the wicked, the common people and their oppressors, salvation and damnation.[25]

It was obvious to all pietists who listened that Bryan was one of them, that he saw the world in the terms in which they saw it. For those of a different religious perspective, the message was just as clear.

The election of 1896 represents one way that specific presidential candidacies can take on particular religious significance. One other example should be mentioned here. Analysis of the election of 1928 makes it clear that a presidential candidacy can take on special religious relevance in a very different way. In this case, the mere fact of Al Smith's Catholicism, and all that this religious identification represented to both Protestants and Catholics, seemed to alter the voting patterns of a great many Americans. The basic tendency of Protestants to vote Republican and Catholics to vote Democratic was intensified and, unlike in 1896, this effect was of long-term duration.[26]

It is obvious, even from these few examples, that there are a number of ways that a presidential candidacy can enhance the relationship between religion and voting behavior. We shall keep this in mind when we begin our analysis of the modern political period.

Religion and Status Displacement

> Proposition: All other things being equal, the tendency of a religious group to use political action to achieve its religious goals will be positively related to its feelings of status displacement. Status displacement will therefore increase the influence of religion on voting behavior.

While the rise and fall in the importance of religion as a factor affecting voting behavior can be partially explained through changes at the elite level, something else seems to be at work. An examination of American history suggests that changes at the mass level have also played an important role in this ever-changing relationship. One such type of mass-level change involves the concept of "status displacement," which has been the centerpiece of a number of sociological studies that are of relevance here. Perhaps the most important of these is the work of Seymour Martin Lipset. In his massive study, Lipset attempted to explain the rise and fall of right-wing political movements throughout the nation's history. Although his focus was on right-wing movements in general, his conclusions have important implications for explaining variations in the religious factor over time.[27]

One of the generalizations that can be derived from our examination of the presurvey period is that the various religious groups have not been equally likely to initiate political action. Usually it has been the conservative Protestants who have been the most willing to utilize government action as a means of achieving their religious goals. Often this has meant that other groups, such as Catholics and Jews, have been forced to resort to politics as a means of cultural defense. Therefore, if we can succeed in explaining this affinity for political action among this religious right, and why it varies over time, we will have moved a long way toward understanding the overall pattern of religious-political change.

Status displacement may provide a key to this understanding. According to Lipset, the origin of right-wing political movements can largely be traced to the massive economic, social, and demographic changes that have been so much a part of American history. These changes differentially affect various segments of the population, resulting in gains for some groups at the expense of others. Sensing a decline in their relative social status, the disadvantaged groups become highly motivated to use the instruments of government policy as a means of halting or reversing, what are for them, adverse trends. This preservatist thrust is the heart of right-wing extremist politics.[28]

While the present study is not concerned with right-wing movements in general, Lipset's general theory would seem to be of use in explaining why conservative Protestant groups become unusually politicized at certain points in time. Significantly, most of the right-wing extremist movements that Lipset examined incorporated a conservative Protestant religious base. This fundamentalist Protestantism added strength to the movements by providing a rather compelling moral dimension. However, Lipset makes it clear that it is not fundamentalism, itself, that is the cause of right-wing movements. The ultimate cause is the status displacement of the group or groups on which the movement is based.[29] For our purposes, the message is clear. If we are to explain the way that conservative religious movements are transformed into conservative political movements (become politicized), we must seek to understand the reasons for the feelings of status displacement among the members of the groups involved.

In order to accomplish this task it is, of course, critical that we start by clarifying exactly what is meant by status displacement. Lipset's definition of status displacement is a very broad one. "This construct of the genesis of political extremism is not tied to any of the technical definitions of status deprivation. The variety of the states of disaffection that have attended right-wing extremist movements in America defies the monopoly of any particularistic definition."[30] Status displacement can result from changes in income, occupation, education, group percentage of the population, or more subtle changes in accepted values and standards.

Because of the breadth of this definition, it is perhaps useful to point out the various ways that the word "status" has been defined by other scholars who have invoked it in their attempts to explain the causes of right-wing extremist movements. Page and Clelland draw attention to these definitional distinctions in their critique of past research on status politics. Specifically, the term "status" can be used in two different ways. According to the first definition, status refers to social prestige while status politics refers to the kinds of social conflict that flow out of changes in the relative prestige of various societal groups.[31] An example of a work using this type of definition is Gusfield's study of the Women's Christian Temperance Union (WCTU). When it was founded in the late nineteenth century, the WCTU was dominated mainly by a middle- and upper-middle-class leadership and its temperance ethic was combined with broader humanitarian efforts at social welfare. Temperance was seen not just as a moral issue but as a key solution to poverty and a way of bringing the working classes into middle-class Protestant society. As time went on and middle-class views on drinking began to moderate, these more socially prestigious leaders began to withdraw from the organization, leaving the lower classes in charge. Whereas membership in the WCTU had once offered a kind of social prestige, it now became open to ridicule by the larger society. This loss of status by the remaining membership caused them to strike out in a purely moral condemnation of the upper classes who had deserted them. In short, feelings of loss of social prestige seem to account for the transformation of the WCTU from a fairly broad-based social welfare movement into the narrow and morally rigid organization that it is today.[32]

However, as Page and Clelland point out, there is a second way of defining "status" and "status politics." In this case status refers not to social prestige but to one's style of life. Borrowing from Weber, status groups are seen as basic structural conflict groups, separate from, and crosscutting, economic classes.

> If economic classes may be defined by their relations to the means of production (doing), status groups may be defined in terms of the ends of existence (being). That is, status groups are defined by a common life style, which is more than a set of stylish characteristics which set a social tone and maintain boundaries between prestige groupings. Rather, a status group stands for a way of life; and such groups are consequently involved in constant struggles for control of the means of symbolic production through which their reality is constructed. Such struggles are the essence of status politics.[33]

Page and Clelland then go on to use this version of status politics to explain the conflict over the selection of textbooks in the public schools of Kanawha County, West Virginia, in the mid-1970s. The dispute is seen as a struggle between two life-style groups: cultural modernists and cultural fundamentalists. It is centered around the content of public school textbooks because the school system represents a critical means of symbolic production, through which the younger generation can be brought into one status group or the other. As such, it cuts across economic and educational class lines.[34]

Lipset's definition would seem to be broad enough to encompass both of these versions of status conflict. Right-wing extremist movements may result from a threat to a group's social prestige or its basic style of life. Consequently, we shall not limit ourselves to one or another of these definitions. In attempting to explain the apparent entry of the religious right into American politics in the last few years, we shall search for any possible status threat that could be operating as a motivating factor, whether this involves some observable loss of social prestige or more subtle cultural changes that could lead this group to feel that its basic style of life is somehow under seige.

Before we move on to our final section, however, it seems worthwhile to offer one example of exactly how Lipset used the concept of status displacement to explain the rise and fall of right-wing extremism in American history. As mentioned in the first section, the decade of 1920s was one of rising right-wing activity in many parts of the country. During this period, membership in the Ku Klux Klan (KKK) rose to between 3 and 6 million.

> In those terms, restricted as it was to the adult native-born Protestant male, active KKK membership blanketed about 15 to 20 percent of the total adult male population and 25 to 30 percent of the Protestant population. It dominated "for a time the seven states of Oregon, Oklahoma, Texas, Arkansas, Indiana, Ohio, and California." It also had considerable strength in the rest of the South, other states in the Midwest, and Maine.[35]

The core ideology of this right-wing extremism was fundamentalist Protestantism. By 1920 this style of life was on the decline. The threat to this traditional Protestant culture took a number of forms, among which were the rapid industrialization and urbanization that the country was undergoing at that time.

> The city had never been the center of the previously predominant evangelical Protestant culture. The two major evangelical and

moralistic denominations, the Methodists and the Baptists, had formed a majority of American Protestantism since early in the nineteenth century, but both groups had been rooted in small towns and rural areas.

In addition to this, the previous decades had seen the influx of millions of Catholic and Jewish immigrants. White Protestants had come to find themselves a numerical minority in the large metropolitan areas of the country.[36]

In this case, Lipset was able to find a number of different threats to the status of fundamentalist Protestant groups. Demographic changes were rapidly making them a numerical minority in many areas of the country. Industrialization and urbanization provided new social realities that offered potential obstacles to the preservation of traditional Protestant culture. Faced with these adverse social, economic, and demographic trends, many conservative Protestants became more and more willing to use the powers of the state to protect themselves from any further status decline.

Fundamentalist Protestantism

In explaining the rise of right-wing extremist movements in American history, Lipset attributed ultimate causality to status displacement. Nevertheless, his model does not ignore the role that fundamentalist Protestantism played in many of these preservatist campaigns. This orthodox Christianity provided such movements with an important moral justification for actions that were, in reality, designed to protect the interests of those involved. From this perspective, fundamentalism is seen as a form of "cultural baggage" rather than as a prime motivational factor in itself.

> Thus religious fundamentalism and fanaticism is seen primarily as the specific symbolic content of lost-group status, of the Quondom Complex, rather than as a kind of intellectual mind-set which is the direct source of right wing extremism. Since the defense of ascribed group status must also be made on a moralistic basis, the use of moral and religious dimensions as the "remembered elements of culture" is particularly appropriate.[37]

Lipset's attempt was to develop a general social theory that would apply equally to all social groups. As such, the exact nature of the religious beliefs of the specific group under threat was of little consequence.

> Again, people or groups who are the objects rather than the bene-ficiaries of change tend to seek a general "fundamentalism" in order, as Paul Tillich put it, "to have a principle which transcends their whole disintegrated existence in individual and social life." But that kind of generic fundamentalism, which would also have to be found if it did not exist, does not have to take the form of religious, much less Protestant, conservatism.[38]

It is on this point that we will part company with the theory of Lipset. While placing emphasis on status displacement, it is our contention that the religious beliefs of the specific groups being displaced play an independent causal role in determining whether or not they will seek government action as a means of reversing their status decline. Specifically, we will argue that the content of fundamentalist Protestant theology makes its adherents partic-ularly predisposed to attempt to use government policy as a means of enforcing their version of social morality. Thus, when a status threat in some way involves this sense of morality, their theological predisposition will greatly increase the likelihood that a preservatist political movement will form.

In order to better understand this conservative Protestant view of social morality, it seems worthwhile to examine briefly its historical development. One of the earliest scholars to attempt to trace this development and its implications for social behavior was Max Weber. Weber's famous explanation for the rise of modern capitalism in the Western world centered heavily around the Calvinist emphasis on individual morality and personal asceticism. This em-phasis on individual conduct flowed in turn from Calvin's doctrine of predestination. At first glance, this link between doctrine and conduct would seem to make little sense. Predestination meant that the spiritual fate of each individual had already been deter-mined prior to this birth. Consequently, there was nothing that a person could do to affect his own destiny. However, this uncer-tainty was too much for faithful Calvinists to bear. They began to seek reassurance of their salvation through ascetic service to God, while still in this world. Thus, the end result of the doctrine was to raise concern with moral behavior to a level that had not existed prior to the beginning of the reformation.[39]

Weber's emphasis on the individualistic element in Calvinism was later to come under attack by R. H. Tawney. Tawney suggested that Calvinist doctrine actually incorporated two distinct and somewhat contradictory components. "The two main elements in this teaching were the insistence on personal responsibility, discipline, and asceticism, and the call to fashion for the Christian character an objective embodiment in social institutions. Though logically connected, they were often in practical discord." It is the latter element, the emphasis on social morality, that forms one important basis for modern fundamentalist Protestantism. This "Christian Socialism" was to take material form with the founding of the Calvinist experiments in collectivist theocracy at Geneva, and later at Colonial Massachusetts.[40]

Orthodox Calvinism, however, was not to survive in the American context. The conditions of the frontier society provided stresses that were to lead to the development of a new religious form, evangelism.

> Another feature, present before 1750 but now accentuated (by 1800), was emphasis upon 'evangelism,' the seeking to win every individual to allegiance to Christ. From the standpoint of the churches this was especially important in view of the fact that there was no legal requirement of membership and that a large majority of the population were not formally connected with any church and were in danger of being de-Christianized. In such bodies as the Congregationalists, Baptists, Methodists, and most Presbyterians, in other words those comprising the large majority of the church members of the country, personal conversion was stressed.[41]

However, this emphasis on salvation through individual conversion ran headlong into the doctrine of predestination, which taught that the decision on one's spiritual fate had already been made. Gradually this notion of the "elect" was modified and ultimately abandoned by most of the American denominations. However, the old Calvinist emphasis on collective morality, which had been introduced to the new world by the Puritans, remained largely in place. "There was also a trend in some denominations, in part the heritage from the Quakers and the founders of New England, to seek to make all society conform to Christian standards. After 1815 this was to issue in many reform movements."[42]

In sum, the doctrines of the Calvinist churches, which took many forms but which all placed heavy emphasis on sin and collective morality, became transformed when faced with the unique social conditions of American frontier society. These conditions led to the abandonment of the doctrine of predestination and the emergence of a new stress on personal conversion and evangelism. This evangelism was combined with the surviving emphasis on sin and social morality to form the basis of what is now called fundamentalist Protestantism.

It is exactly this religious perspective that historians Paul Kleppner and Richard Jensen characterized as pietistic, in their separate investigations of the religious divisions that formed the basis of much of the partisan conflict of the late nineteenth century. Pietism emphasized evangelism and the sinfulness of man.

> Its concentration on conversion, a change of heart, personal piety, and a relative informality in worship characterize it as an active orientation. Though seeing the world as a sinful one, it does not accept that condition but concerns itself with converting people, with helping them to make the change from a life of sin to one of "being saved."[43]

In addition, pietists believed in the importance of social morality. "The bridge linking theology and politics was the demand by pietists that the government remove the major obstacle to the purification of society through revivalistic Christianity, institutionalized immorality."[44]

This brief examination of the roots of fundamentalist Protestantism should make it clear that the idea of using government to achieve religious ends flows directly from fundamentalist theology. Consequently, we have chosen to view this theology as an independent causal factor that, along with status displacement, may act to motivate preservatist political behavior. In order to explain the politicization of religion, we will search for status changes among the groups involved; but status displacement is not in itself an adequate explanation. If status changes were to threaten equally the basic values of all the major American religious groups, we would expect the conservative Protestants to be the most likely to turn to political action as a means of reversing, what are for them, unfavorable social trends.

This completes the development of our theoretical propositions concerning the nature of religious-political change. Having done this, our first step toward testing them must be the development of a valid measure of religious values and beliefs. Such will be the task of Chapter 2.

NOTES

1. Seymour Martin Lipset, *Revolution and Counterrevolution: Change and Persistence in Social Structures* (Garden City, N.Y.: Doubleday, 1970), p. 308.

2. Ibid.

3. Ibid.

4. Ibid., p. 309.

5. Ibid., p. 311.

6. Ibid., p. 312.

7. Ibid., p. 314.

8. Ibid.

9. Ibid., p. 315.

10. Ibid., pp. 315-18.

11. Seymour Martin Lipset and Earl Raab, *The Politics of Unreason: Right Wing Extremism in America, 1790-1977* (Chicago: University of Chicago Press, 1978), p. 48.

12. Paul Kleppner, *The Cross of Culture: A Social Analysis of Midwestern Politics, 1850-1900* (New York: The Free Press, 1970), p. 6.

13. Ibid., p. 73.

14. Ibid., p. 372.

15. Richard Jensen, *The Winning of the Midwest: Social and Political Conflict, 1888-1896* (Chicago: University of Chicago Press, 1971).

16. Kleppner, Chapter 8.

17. Lipset, p. 329.

18. James L. Sundquist, *Dynamics of the Party System: Alignment and Realignment of Political Parties in the United States* (Washington D.C.: The Brookings Institution, 1973), p. 153.

19. Lipset, p. 331.

20. Lipset and Raab, pp. 110-17.

21. Lipset, p. 331.

22. Ibid., p. 334.

23. Ibid., pp. 335-42.

24. Kleppner, Chapter 8.

25. Jensen, p. 276.

26. Lipset, p. 334.

27. Lipset and Raab.

28. Ibid.

29. Ibid., p. 118.

30. Ibid., p. 487.

31.   Ann Page and Donald Clelland, "The Kanawha County Textbook Controversy: A Study of the Politics of Life Style Concern," *Social Forces* 57 (September 1978).

32.   Joseph Gusfield, "Social Structure and Moral Reform: A Study of the Women's Christian Temperance Union," *American Journal of Sociology* 61 (November 1955): 221-32.

33.   Page and Clelland, p. 266.

34.   Ibid., p. 267.

35.   Lipset and Raab, p. 111.

36.   Ibid., pp. 113-14.

37.   Ibid., p. 488.

38.   Ibid., p. 118.

39.   Max Weber, *The Protestant Ethic and the Spirit of Capitalism* (New York: Charles Scribner's Sons, 1958 [originally 1904-05]).

40.   R. H. Tawney, *Religion and the Rise of Capitalism: A Historical Study* (Gloucester, Mass.: Harcourt, Brace and World, 1962 [originally 1926]), pp. 112-13.

41.   Kenneth Scott Latourette, *A History of Christianity* (New York: Harper and Row, 1953), pp. 1045-46.

42.   Ibid., p. 1046.

43.   Kleppner, p. 73.

44.   Jensen, p. 67.

2

Measuring Religious Values and Beliefs

INTRODUCTION

The study of history teaches us of the complexity of human behavior. Mankind is motivated by so many factors, both external and internal to himself, that it sometimes seems an impossible task to begin to sort them all out. Among these factors are the basic beliefs of individuals concerning the nature of the world around them. Man seeks to understand, but to a greater or lesser degree the world withholds its secrets from him. Not content with the awareness of his own ignorance, he will often seek to fill the gaps in his knowledge with the substance of faith. This process lies at the heart of those great systems of beliefs and values that have become known as religions.

The critically important role that religious beliefs and values have played in human history can hardly be denied. Religion has at various points in time been known to inspire acts of war and peace, revolution and subjugation, censorship and the pursuit of knowledge. Yet as societies have modernized, the influence of religion on people's lives seems to have declined. Among other things, this process of secularization has meant that the links between religious beliefs and various forms of human behavior have been weakened. In fact, large portions of the populations of the advanced industrial states seem to have rejected any kind of traditional religious beliefs altogether.

The first task of this chapter, then is to attempt to provide evidence that, at least in the American case, this process of religious decline has not advanced to a level that would render meaningless our attempt to link religious beliefs with political behavior. Fortunately, such evidence does exist. In the mid-1970s, several Gallup surveys were undertaken in an attempt to measure the level of religious decline in a number of advanced industrial democracies. The findings were compared with those from similar surveys taken in various years since 1948. Not surprisingly, the percentage of citizens responding affirmatively to a number of questions on religious belief declined significantly in a number of the countries studied. The major exception to this trend was the United States. "The United States stands at the top of the industrialized societies in the importance religion plays in the lives of its citizens. The findings from the global study, when compared with earlier surveys, show the level of belief and practice to have remained more or less constant among the American people, while something approaching a collapse of faith may be occurring in certain European and other nations of the world."[1]

Some of these findings are presented in Table 2.1. The first question simply asked respondents how important they consider their religious beliefs to be in their lives. Table 2.1 lists the percentage in each country who consider these beliefs to be "very important." In the United States 58 percent gave this particular

TABLE 2.1
Religious Beliefs in Western Nations

Country	Percent Responding "Very Important"	Percent Believing in God or Universal Spirit	Percent Believing in Life after Death
United States	58	94	71
Italy	36	88	46
Canada	36	89	54
Benelux	26	78	48
Australia	25	80	48
United Kingdom	23	76	43
France	22	72	39
West Germany	17	72	33
Scandinavia	17	65	35

Source: George Gallup, "Religion at Home and Abroad," *Public Opinion*, March-May 1979, pp. 38-39.

response, well above the percentage for the second highest country, Italy, for which the figure is 36 percent. The Scandinavian countries and West Germany rank the lowest, with only 17 percent of each population responding in this manner.

The other two questions asked respondents about specific religious beliefs. The first of these asked whether or not the individual believes in God or a universal spirit. In this case the United States also ranks first with a full 94 percent of respondents answering in the affirmative. This percentage has remained "more or less constant over the last quarter century." Such is not the case with a number of the other countries surveyed. For instance, in the seven years from 1968 to 1975 the percentage of Scandinavians believing in God dropped from 81 percent to 65 percent, while the West Germans showed a nine-point drop during the same period.[2]

The final question attempted to measure the percentage of respondents who believe in life after death. Once again Americans lead with 71 percent expressing such a belief, well above the 54 percent for the second highest country, Canada. As with belief in God, the American figure has remained fairly stable since 1948, while many other nations have shown a marked decline. In the same 27-year period, this decline has amounted to 34 percent for Canadians, 20 percent for the Benelux countries, and 26 percent for Scandinavians.[3]

Two facts become obvious from Table 2.1. The first is that the forces of secularization have not affected Americans in the same way that they have affected the populations of other Western countries in the years since World War II. This peculiarity is difficult to explain, but we can speculate as to the reason. Each of the countries surveyed has a strong Christian heritage, yet the form that Christianity has taken has not been uniform from one to another. Specifically, the fact of being a "Christian" in America has not had the same meaning it has long had in many of the European nations. In Europe the link between church and state has historically been quite strong, and membership in one or another church has taken on a formal, even legal, meaning. On the other hand, the lack of an official state church and the plethora of Christian denominations in America have forced Americans to view Christianity in more subjective terms. It may have been the case that the belief structures among European populations were much more dependent on formal church institutions, which long played an important role in so many aspects of European life. Modernization has brought the weakening of these formal church structures as the churches have been forced to retreat into much narrower roles within the societies they once dominated. The American churches, on the other hand, have had a much longer time to adapt to these limits and to develop the mechanisms through which they can influence the religious beliefs of individuals, without the benefit of an all-pervasive formal church structure. The American emphasis on personal conversion, mentioned in Chapter 1, is consistent with this idea.

However, for our purposes, the second fact made obvious by Table 2.1 is of greater importance. This is the empirical validation of the idea that, at least in the realm of belief, Americans are still a highly religious people. This, of course, allows for the possibility that religious beliefs do in fact have a major impact on the political behavior of the American citizenry. Before attempting to test this idea, however, we must develop a realistic way of measuring these religious beliefs.

DENOMINATION AND RELIGIOUS BELIEF

In their seminal work in the sociology of religion, Rodney Stark and Charles Glock asserted that the various forms of religious commitment expressed by the American public fall along four separate dimensions: belief, practice, experience, and knowledge. Though any single individual may partake in more than one religious form, it was demonstrated that among the mass sample under study the four dimensions showed a strong statistical independence from one another.[4] Although each is important in its own right, it is the belief dimension that is of greatest concern to our study. Among the vast array of beliefs that individuals hold about the universe around them, religious beliefs tend to be among the most central. This gives them a psychological role of such great importance that, once adopted, they can affect other, less central beliefs and the behavior that stems from them. For most Americans these less central beliefs include their political orientations. It can be expected, then, that for a great many individuals religious beliefs affect political behavior.

One characteristic of American Christianity that sets it apart from that of other Western nations is its degree of pluralism. American history has witnessed the development of a wide variety of religious denominations that claim the title of "Christian." Aside from differences in organizational structure, the thing that most separates any one of these denominations from all the others is the unique blend of specific doctrines that it claims as religious truth. Those affiliated with each denomination are supposed to adhere to its particular version of proper doctrine. If this is in fact the case, it allows for the possibility that knowledge of an individual's denominational affiliation will tell us a great deal about his actual religious beliefs.

The first step toward the development of a denominational indicator of religious beliefs must, therefore, be the empirical validation of meaningful denominational differences. Fortunately, such empirical evidence does exist in the form of Stark and Glock's masterful study. Using both national and California church-member samples, they were able to show that the percentage of respondents adhering to each of a number of specific religious beliefs varies widely from one denomination to another.[5] A close examination of their findings should indicate their potential relevance to our study.

Perhaps the most basic element of all the major Western religions is the belief in an all-powerful personal God. As indicated earlier, virtually all Americans reply affirmatively when confronted with a simple either/or question about this particular religious doctrine. However, put in such a simple fashion, this type of question may actually hide a high degree of variance among the American public regarding individual conceptions of God, as well as variations in certainty of belief. In order to avoid this oversimplification, Stark and Glock presented respondents with a number of statements concerning the nature of God and asked them to indicate the statement with which they most agreed. The results of this effort are presented in Table 2.2, which gives the percentage of respondents from each denomination who agreed with each of the specific statements. The data are taken from the California church-member study conducted in 1963.[6]

The first of these responses expresses a certainty of belief in a personal God. It can be seen immediately that a large majority of respondents agree with this most emphatic expression of faith in a Supreme Being. Of greater interest, however, is the variance found across denominations. Only about two in five Congregationalists are certain of the existence of a personal God. At the other end of the spectrum, virtually all of the Southern Baptists and

TABLE 2.2
Belief in God

"Which of the following statements comes closest to what you believe about God?"

A. I know God really exists and I have no doubts about it.
B. While I have doubts, I feel that I do believe in God.
C. I find myself believing in God some of the time, but not at other times.
D. I don't believe in a personal God, but I believe in a higher power of some kind.
E. I don't know whether there is a God and I don't believe there is any way to find out.
F. I don't believe in God.
G. No answer.

Denomination	A	B	C	D	E	F	G
				(in percentages)			
Congregational	41	34	4	16	2	1	2
Methodist	60	22	4	11	2	*	*
Episcopalian	63	19	2	12	2	*	1
Disciples of Christ	76	20	0	0	0	0	4
Presbyterian	75	16	1	7	1	0	*
American Lutheran	73	19	2	6	*	0	*
American Baptist	78	18	0	2	0	0	2
Missouri Lutheran	81	17	0	1	1	0	0
Southern Baptist	99	1	0	0	0	0	0
Sects†	96	2	0	1	0	0	1
Total Protestant	71	17	2	7	1	*	1
Roman Catholic	81	13	1	3	1	0	1

*Less than 0.5 percent.

†The sects include The Assemblies of God, The Church of God, The Church of Christ, The Church of the Nazarene, The Foursquare Gospel Church, and one independent tabernacle.

Source: The source for tables 2.2 through 2.7 is Rodney Stark and Charles Y. Glock, *American Piety: The Nature of Religious Commitment* (Berkeley: University of California Press, 1968).

Sect members respond in this manner. The differences found between Protestants and Catholics are much smaller than those found
among the various Protestant groups. These denominational differences were largely confirmed by a national survey of the general
public taken 18 months later, thus precluding the possibility that
denominational differences are meaningful only among those who
hold formal church membership. Psychological attachment to one
or another denomination, rather than formal organizational membership, seems to be the key differentiating factor.[7]

While belief in a personal God is something common to each
of the major Western religious traditions, there are other specific
beliefs that help to define an individual as a "Christian." Perhaps
the most critical of these is the belief in the divinity of Jesus Christ.
While others, such as the Moslems, acknowledge the existence of
Jesus as prophet and teacher, only Christians accept the notion
of the trinity as a basic tenet of faith. Each of the major Christian
denominations in America includes this tenet in its official doctrine.
Nevertheless, we can expect that, as with belief in a personal God,
variations among denominations in the acceptance of this belief
will exist. Such expectations are borne out by the data presented
in Table 2.3. Once again, only about two out of five Congregationalists express absolute certainty regarding this doctrine, which is
of central importance to traditional Christianity. In the middle
ranges, roughly three-fourths of American Lutherans and American
Baptists adhere to this position, while almost all of the Southern
Baptists and Sect members do so.[8]

Table 2.4 presents findings concerning another aspect of traditional Christian doctrine, belief in Biblical miracles. Of greatest
interest is the percentage of respondents from each denomination
who express certainty of belief in a literal interpretation of such
Biblical phenomena. The Bible is far and away the centerpiece of
Christian teaching and the way that it is interpreted is a key factor
differentiating one Christian group from another. It is probably
fair to say that for a modern American, living in a society that
places tremendous emphasis on scientific method and a rational-
skeptical approach to acquiring knowledge, miraculous accounts
of the suspension of the laws of nature can be somewhat difficult
to accept. Therefore, this particular indicator would seem to provide
us with an important measure of the survival of traditional Christianity in the present-day United States. The findings indicate
that acceptance of this belief varies widely across the Protestant

denominations, with Catholics falling near the center of the spectrum. Only about one in four Congregationalists accepts this particular article of faith, while acceptance among Southern Baptists and sect members is, once again, nearly unanimous.[9]

Finally, Table 2.5 presents findings concerning two other important tenets of traditional Christianity: life after death and the existence of the Devil. These two beliefs are important underpinnings of the doctrine of spiritual salvation. According to this traditional view, an individual moves through life facing one temptation after another. Behind these temptations lies a powerful and

TABLE 2.3
Belief in the Divinity of Jesus

"Which of the following statements comes closest to what you believe about Jesus?"

A. Jesus is the Divine Son of God and I have no doubts about it.
B. While I have some doubts, I feel basically that Jesus is Divine.
C. I feel that Jesus was a great man and very holy, but I don't feel Him to be the Son of God any more than all of us are children of God.
D. I think Jesus was only a man, although an extraordinary one.
E. Frankly, I'm not entirely sure there was such a person as Jesus.
F. Other and no answer.

Denomination	A	B	C	D	E	F
			(in percentages)			
Congregational	40	28	19	9	1	3
Methodist	54	22	14	6	1	3
Episcopalian	59	25	8	5	1	2
Disciples of Christ	74	14	6	2	0	4
Presbyterian	72	19	5	2	1	1
American Lutheran	74	18	5	3	*	0
American Baptist	76	16	4	2	0	2
Missouri Lutheran	93	5	0	1	0	1
Southern Baptist	99	0	0	1	0	0
Sects	97	2	*	*	0	1
Total Protestant	69	17	7	4	1	2
Roman Catholic	86	8	3	1	0	2

*Less than 0.5 percent.

sinister force in the person of the Devil, who is the root of all evil. The individual's success in overcoming such temptation, with the aid of Christ, will determine the spiritual fate of his soul after his death. It is not surprising that the distribution of denominational scores on each of these two measures of Christian traditionalism follows the basic pattern of the other three, with Congregationalists and Methodists holding down the skeptical end of the spectrum while Southern Baptists and sect members hold down the other end. As with all the other measures that we have examined, Roman Catholics fall near the middle.[10]

It seems worth pausing for a moment to consider how these data compare with the findings of the historical studies mentioned in Chapter 1. It quickly becomes evident that certain Protestant

TABLE 2.4
Miracles

"The Bible tells of miracles, some credited to Christ and some to other prophets and apostles. Generally speaking, which of the following statements comes closest to what you believe about Biblical miracles?"

A. Miracles actually happened just as the Bible says they did.
B. Miracles happened but can be explained by natural causes.
C. Doubt or do not accept miracles.

Denomination	A	B (in percentages)	C
Congregational	28	32	32
Methodist	37	31	24
Episcopalian	41	22	27
Disciples of Christ	62	16	14
Presbyterian	58	20	14
American Lutheran	69	14	13
American Baptist	62	16	9
Missouri Lutheran	89	4	5
Southern Baptist	92	0	3
Sects	92	3	5
Total Protestant	57	19	17
Roman Catholic	74	9	9

Note: Figures do not add up to 100 percent due to missing data.

TABLE 2.5
Life beyond Death/The Devil

The percent who responded "completely true" to the following statements:

A. There is a life beyond death.
B. The Devil actually exists.

Denomination	A	B
		(in percentages)
Congregational	36	6
Methodist	49	13
Episcopalian	53	17
Disciples of Christ	64	18
Presbyterian	69	31
American Lutheran	70	49
American Baptist	72	49
Missouri Lutheran	84	77
Southern Baptist	97	92
Sects	94	90
Total Protestant	65	38
Roman Catholic	75	66

denominations have changed radically over time. In the early years of the republic the Congregationalist church still bore powerful remnants of its Calvinist heritage, putting great emphasis on sin and social morality. In fact it was the main force behind many of the earliest attempts to use government to strengthen public morality. By the 1960s this particular denomination had evolved to a point where a majority of its members either expressed doubt about or rejected outright each of the traditional Christian beliefs measured in the Stark and Glock study. Another group that underwent a significant evolution of belief was the Methodists. During the nineteenth century the Methodists stood as one of the key fundamentalist Protestant denominations in America. By the 1960s they had moved far away from the other major fundamentalist groups, such as the Southern Baptists and small sects, in their adherence to key tenets of Christian orthodoxy. One final interesting fact is the distinction in belief between Southern Baptists and American Baptists. These two groups had originally existed in one unified body, dividing over the slave issue just prior to the Civil

War. Once divided, they seem to have moved away from one another, with Southern Baptists now being much more willing to accept traditional Christian beliefs than their American Baptist counterparts.

Each of the beliefs that we have examined thus far measures one aspect of what is often referred to as orthodox Christianity. In order to develop a summary measure of where each of the American denominations stands in relation to this orthodoxy, Stark and Glock developed an orthodoxy index, which combines scores on individual items concerning the existence of a personal God, the divinity of Jesus Christ, the authenticity of Biblical miracles, and the existence of the Devil. Each respondent received a score of 1 for each belief item on which he expressed a certainty of the truth of the orthodox Christian position. Thus the index ranges from a score of 4 (the perfect orthodox position) to a score of 0 (the position of perfect doubt or disbelief). Table 2.6 displays the differences among denominations on this overall orthodoxy index. Those scoring at the high end of the scale range from a mere 4 percent of Congregationalists and 10 percent of Methodists to an impressive 88 percent of Southern Baptists and 86 percent of sect members.[11] It becomes obvious that denominational affiliation is a powerful predictor of orthodox Christian beliefs.

TABLE 2.6
Orthodoxy Index
(in percentages)

Denomination	High-4	3	2	1	0-Low
Congregational	4	18	18	12	48
Methodist	10	20	23	17	30
Episcopalian	14	23	21	18	24
Disciples of Christ	18	36	23	7	16
Presbyterian	27	29	16	12	16
American Lutheran	43	20	12	12	13
American Baptist	43	20	18	7	12
Missouri Lutheran	66	21	7	5	1
Southern Baptist	88	9	3	0	0
Sects	86	10	3	0	1
Total Protestant	33	21	16	12	18
Roman Catholic	62	19	6	4	9

We can see, then, that the various major Protestant denominations in America can be arrayed on a spectrum ranging from liberal to conservative. Those at the conservative end adhere to a basic orthodox Christian belief system, while those at the liberal end have, to one degree or another, moved away from this orthodoxy. However, it would be a mistake to view liberalism as being simply the lack of orthodoxy. The belief patterns measured by the orthodoxy index deal primarily with the supernatural world and man's relationship to it, but there is another side to Christianity. For many, the primary message to be derived from the New Testament concerns not so much man's relationship to the supernatural, but rather his relationship to his fellow man. This perspective emphasizes adherence to a set of ethical principles that are intended to make life on earth more pleasant for all of mankind. It is exactly this perspective that is measured by Stark and Glock's ethicalism index, which combines responses to two separate items that ask respondents to rate the importance of "doing good for others" and "loving thy neighbor" as requirements for salvation. Christians scoring high on this index place great emphasis on ethical behavior as a requirement for achieving salvation after death, while those scoring low express the belief that such behavior is unrelated to salvation. Table 2.7 displays the denominational breakdown on this ethicalism index. The findings are most intriguing. Although the pattern is not as clear-cut as it was for the orthodoxy index, there is a definite tendency for the liberal Protestant denominations to place more emphasis on ethicalism than their conservative counterparts. The one major exception to the pattern is the sects. Members of these tiny groups display a surprising amount of concern with ethical behavior. However, upon looking more closely, Stark and Glock discovered the reason for this anomaly. Sect members tend to be so preoccupied with achieving salvation that they believe that "everything" has a bearing on it. Making the findings all the more impressive is the fact that the differences among denominations regarding their emphasis on ethical behavior are probably understated, since many members of the liberal denominations reject the concept of salvation altogether. Such individuals scored low on the ethicalism index. Thus, the overall scores of the liberal groups are misleadingly low.[12]

Among Protestant denominations, then, there is an inverse correlation between adherence to orthodox beliefs and emphasis on ethicalism. Those denominations that emphasize one tend to deemphasize the other.[13] With this in mind, we can now properly define the terms liberal and conservative in relation to the Protestant spectrum. The conservative Protestant denominations tend to place emphasis on adherence to a set of orthodox beliefs as requirements for salvation, while deemphasizing the need for "man-to-man ethicalism." The liberal denominations tend to deemphasize orthodox beliefs, and many in them reject the concept of salvation altogether. On the other hand, these groups place great emphasis on such ethical commands as "loving thy neighbor" and "doing good for others."

Thus, the Protestant denominations can be said to differ along two basic dimensions. The first measures degree of adherence to traditional beliefs about the supernatural, while the second measures degree of emphasis on man's obligations to other men. There is no logical requirement for these two dimensions to be inversely correlated, yet empirical evidence indicates that among American Protestant groups this is in fact the case. Though the two dimensions are conceptually distinct, the fact that the denominations tend to fall in the same order on each allows us to speak meaningfully of a single Protestant spectrum.

But where do Catholics stand in relation to this spectrum? In order to answer this question we must determine where Catholics fall on each of these two dimensions and how the dimensions are

TABLE 2.7
Ethicalism Index
(in percentages)

Denomination	High-4	Medium-3,2	Low-1,0
Congregational	52	42	6
Methodist	51	45	4
Episcopalian	51	45	4
Disciples of Christ	60	40	0
Presbyterian	43	46	11
American Lutheran	41	43	16
American Baptist	43	41	16
Missouri Lutheran	37	41	22
Southern Baptist	33	27	40
Sects	61	32	7
Total Protestant	48	42	10
Roman Catholic	53	45	2

related to one another. On the Orthodoxy index Catholics tend to score rather high. Treated as a single denomination, they fall somewhere in between the conservative Protestant groups such as the Southern Baptists and the moderate groups such as the American Lutherans and the American Baptists. On individual items, Catholics tend to express strong belief in a personal God, in the divinity of Jesus Christ, in a literal interpretation of Biblical miracles, in life after death, and in the existence of the Devil. However, on the ethicalism index Catholics also tend to rank near the top. In fact, among Catholics there is a slight positive correlation between orthodoxy and ethicalism. "Those higher on ethicalism are slightly more likely to be highly orthodox than are those lower on ethicalism. This suggests that the emphasis given by the Catholic church to the social (as opposed to personal) responsibilities of the proper Christian has borne some fruit. For Catholics, adherence to traditional orthodoxy is not entirely at the expense of the traditional ethics of the Sermon on the Mount."[14]

Among Catholics, then, the two belief dimensions, orthodoxy and ethicalism, are positively related. This fact is reason enough to treat Catholics as a separate religious group, independent of the Protestant spectrum. There is no meaningful way to place Catholics on this spectrum. There are, of course, other reasons for keeping Catholics as a separate religious category. Although Catholics rank near conservative Protestants in their adherence to orthodox Christian beliefs, there are important differences between these two groups regarding the way that they view the meaning of religious faith. We shall elaborate on these differences in the next section. In addition, it is possible that the unique historical experiences of American Catholics, as a minority Christian group in a Christian country, have affected the way that they translate religious beliefs into political behavior.

THE DENOMINATIONAL CATEGORIES

The findings presented thus far make it clear that denominational affiliation is a meaningful predictor of specific religious beliefs among Christians in present-day United States. There is reason to believe that these differences of faith play an important role in affecting the way that individuals relate to the political world around them. Determining if such a relationship exists is, of course, the main goal of this study.

Before we can begin our analysis, however, a different kind of denominational classification scheme must be developed. The large number of denominations with which Americans identify acts as a barrier to any kind of systematic empirical analysis. This is because the number of cases appearing in each category in a typical national survey sample will be too small to allow for the application of proper statistical controls. In order to get around this hurdle a way must be found to combine specific denominations into larger religious categories.

Fortunately, the findings of Stark and Glock make such a categorization scheme fairly simple to bring about. As suggested earlier, the various Protestant denominations can be meaningfully arrayed on a single spectrum, since they tend to fall in the same order on each of the specific belief questions examined. The major part of our task, then, simply involves finding a way to divide up this Protestant spectrum. A quick glance at the data suggests that certain obvious cutoff points do exist. The Congregationalists, Methodists, and Episcopalians always make up the liberal end of the spectrum. Consequently, we have combined these three groups into our liberal Protestant category. In the same way, the Missouri Synod Lutherans, Southern Baptists, and small sects always hold down the conservative end of the spectrum. These three, taken together, constitute our conservative Protestant category. The remaining denominations in the study have been combined into our moderate Protestant category. Although the order of these moderate denominations on specific belief questions sometimes varies, they always rank in between the liberals and the conservatives. Therefore, such a threefold categorization scheme for Protestants seems justified.[15]

For the reasons mentioned above, Catholics were assigned to a denominational category of their own. The large size of the Catholic church in the United States makes this statistically feasible. This leaves us with a total of four large Christian denominational groups, which constitute the central focus of our study.

The utility of such a categorization scheme stems from the fact that it allows us to move from the politically impoverished Stark and Glock data to other national surveys that focus heavily on political attitudes and behavior. The categorization of respondents by denomination can be repeated for many of these politically oriented studies. One such group of studies for which this is possible is the presidential election survey series conducted every four years by the University of Michigan. These surveys will provide the major source of our data for the remainder of this research effort. Where other survey data are used, the source will be specifically stated.

Now that we have developed our categorization scheme, the first question to be answered involves the distribution of the American population in terms of these religious categories. Table 2.8 presents a denominational breakdown of respondents from the 1980 national election study. As can be readily seen, the four Christian categories of greatest concern to us account for approximately 80 percent of the adult population. The largest of these groups is the Catholics with 23 percent and the smallest is the liberal Protestant with 15 percent. The one out of five Americans who do not fall into any of the four categories include Jews, Eastern Orthodox Christians, members of non-Judeo-Christian religious groups, those who gave no religious preference, and those Protestants who could not be classified.[16]

Since our ultimate concern is with the voting public, in Table 2.9 we have repeated the religious breakdown, this time excluding those who failed to vote in the 1980 presidential election. The findings are not very different from those found for the population as a whole. There is a slight increase in the percentage of liberal and moderate Protestants and a slight drop in the percentage of conservative Protestants. These figures reflect a somewhat lower

TABLE 2.8
A Religious Profile of Americans in 1980

Denominational Category	Percent
Liberal Protestants	15
Moderate Protestants	21
Conservative Protestants	20
Catholics	23
Jews	3
Eastern Orthodox	*
Non-Judeo-Christians	1
No Stated Preference	10
Unclassified Protestants	7
n of cases	1,610

*Less than 0.5 percent.

Source: All of the tables in this chapter were compiled by the author.

TABLE 2.9
A Religious Profile of Americans in 1980, Voters Only

Denominational Category	Percent
Liberal Protestants	17
Moderate Protestants	23
Conservative Protestants	18
Catholics	23
Jews	3
Eastern Orthodox	*
Non-Judeo-Christians	*
No Stated Preference	9
Unclassified Protestants	7
n of cases	955

turnout rate among conservatives than among the other two Protestant groups. The percentage of Catholics remains unchanged.

Table 2.10 repeats the findings of Table 2.9, this time excluding both nonvoters and blacks. The decision to exclude blacks from the analysis is based on two related considerations. The first is that the proportion of black Americans voting Democratic in presidential elections since 1960 has consistently hovered around 90 percent. Therefore, there is little variance from election to election to be explained. Second, there is good reason to believe that this affinity for the Democratic party among black voters is based mainly

TABLE 2.10
A Religious Profile of Americans in 1980, Nonblack Voters Only

Denominational Category	Percent
Liberal Protestants	18
Moderate Protestants	23
Conservative Protestants	16
Catholics	25
Jews	3
Eastern Orthodox	1
Non-Judeo-Christians	*
No Stated Preference	9
Unclassified Protestants	7
n of cases	848

on considerations involving race and the unique problems that the American black population has faced over the last few decades. To the extent that religion influences black voting behavior, it probably does so in connection with these racial considerations. Therefore, the effect of religion on voting behavior will probably by very different for blacks than for other racial groups. This is especially significant in view of the fact that blacks tend to fall disproportionately into the conservative Protestant category, which can be seen by comparing Tables 2.9 and 2.10 (excluding blacks decreases the percentage of conservative Protestants from 18 to 16 percent of the electorate). There is every reason to believe that the effect of religion on black conservative Protestants is very different from its effect on their white conservative Protestant counterparts. Thus, including blacks in our analysis would serve only to distort the findings. For this reason, unless otherwise stated, all our remaining analyses will exclude the black population.

Having examined the distribution of the American population in terms of these religious categories, it seems worthwhile to elaborate a bit further about the differences in religious beliefs that they represent. No actual validation of the category scheme is required since it merely involves the merging of adjacent denominations into larger denominational groups.[17] Therefore the distribution of denominations on the belief scales developed by Stark and Glock should provide us with an accurate picture of the kinds of belief differences to be found among these larger religious categories. There is little to be gained by going back and examining these findings once again.

Nevertheless, the inclusion of additional religious questions in two separate national opinion studies, which were carried out in 1980, should provide us with further insight into these belief differences. The distributions of responses for these latter questions are presented in Table 2.11. The first question, from the Michigan 1980 election survey, asks respondents to designate the statement that most clearly represents their view of how the Bible should be interpreted. The data presented are the percentages of respondents in each denominational category who adhere to a literal interpretation of this important scriptural text. Among Protestants the findings are exactly what we would predict on the basis of the previous findings regarding denominational differences in the acceptance of orthodox Christian beliefs. The scores range from 35 percent for liberals to 72 percent for conservatives, with moderates falling about midway between these two groups. A minor surprise, however, is the fact that Catholics are as likely as liberal Protestants to reject such a literal form of Biblical interpretation. At first this seems to contradict the findings of Stark and Glock. However, upon closer examination it becomes clear that the Stark and Glock measure of Biblical interpretation is quite different from the one used here. The former asked only about belief in Biblical miracles, while the latter attempted to determine an individual's view of the entire Bible. There are a great many things in the Bible, aside from reports of miracles, which may be difficult for a modern American to accept as literal truth (Adam and Eve, the rejection of the theory of evolution, and so on). It seems that many Catholics consider such a literal belief in these other Biblical narratives to be unnecessary to their faith. For these individuals such skepticism does not seem to be inconsistent with their acceptance of the specific tenets of traditional Christianity included in Stark and Glock's orthodoxy index. This finding is consistent with Catholic church doctrine on this subject, which stresses the complexity of the Bible and the need for its interpretation by church officials. Thus, the degree of skepticism shown by Catholics in Table 2.11 does not reflect a general rejection of Christian orthodoxy. On the other hand, this general measure of Biblical literalism helps to highlight an important difference between Catholics and conservative Protestants. It is possible that this difference could, under certain circumstances,

TABLE 2.11

Religious Indicators by Denominational Category in 1980, Nonblacks Only (in percentages)

Denominational Category	Bible Literally True	Had "Born Again" Experience	Tried to Convert Others*
Liberal Protestants	35	28	44
Moderate Protestants	53	36	45
Conservative Protestants	72	61	69
Catholics	35	14	31
n of cases	950	755	1,847

*From Gallup 1980 survey.

have political relevance (regarding such issues as the teaching of "scientific creationism" in public schools).

Of even greater importance, in terms of possible political consequences, are the other two religion measures included in Table 2.11. As can be readily seen from the Stark and Glock data, the two groups most willing to accept orthodox Christian beliefs are the conservative Protestants and the Catholics. Yet this similarity in the substance of their beliefs can be extremely misleading unless we consider an important difference in the way that these two religious groups derive meaning from their faith. For the conservative Protestant, the acquisition of faith is seen as a life-transforming experience that often occurs in a sudden, almost mystical manner. Once an individual receives such faith his spiritual struggle is largely over. Thus, a great distinction is made between those who are "saved" and those who have yet to acquire this all-important state of grace. Consequently, great emphasis is put on the process of conversion or bringing souls to Christ. For Catholics, no such "critical moment" is expected. Instead, life is seen as a constant struggle during which even the most devout are expected to have moments of failing. The role of the church is to offer spiritual strength through the administration of the sacraments, and a means of atonement for sins when even this strength is not enough.

Evidence for this difference in outlook is provided by responses to the last two questions shown in Table 2.11. The first of these, taken from the Michigan survey, asks respondents whether they have ever been "born again" or had a specific conversion experience in their lives. Among Protestants, the percentage responding in the affirmative increases steadily as one moves from liberal to conservative, with by far the biggest gap occurring between the conservative and moderate groups. Catholics, on the other hand, are only half as likely as even the liberal Protestants to report such an experience. The last question, taken from the 1980 Gallup survey, acts as a different sort of measure of this emphasis on conversion or evangelism.[18] In this case respondents were asked if they had ever tried to convert someone else to their faith. Once again, the conservatives are far more likely than the other Protestant groups to acknowledge such an attempt, while the Catholics are much less likely than any of the Protestant groups to do so.

We can now begin to get some idea of the complexity of the situation. When it comes to adherence to basic orthodox Christian beliefs, the Catholics are the group that is most similar to the conservative Protestants. It is possible that, under certain circumstances, this could lead to a similarity in their political behavior. But when it comes to placing emphasis on spreading faith through evangelism, or using acceptance of this faith to distinguish between those that are saved and those that are not, Catholics and conservative Protestants are polar opposites. This latter fact is consistent with the differences in perspective between pietists and liturgicals that we discussed in Chapter 1. Conceivably, it could lead to conflicts between these two groups over the proper role of the state in the regulation of moral behavior, much as it did at other points in American history.

Thus it can be seen that even in matters of faith there are great differences between Catholics and conservative Protestants. These are in addition to the very great differences in their emphasis on ethical behavior. More generally speaking, it is clear that significant differences in belief can be found among all four of our religious categories. In the next section we will develop some hypotheses concerning the ways that such belief differences can lead to differences in political behavior.

RELIGIOUS BELIEFS AND POLITICAL BEHAVIOR

Having completed our examination of the differences in belief among our four major religious categories, we can now turn to our ultimate concern: the way that these belief differences can be expected to impact on presidential voting behavior. We will proceed by examining each of the four groups, one at a time. A summary of the belief findings and their expected political consequences is presented in Table 2.12.

The conservative Protestants tend to rank high in terms of adherence to traditional orthodox Christian beliefs. In addition they score high on evangelism, which means that they are not content with believing themselves, but rather feel compelled to spread these beliefs to others in an effort to save the latter from eternal damnation. However, this concern with acting out their Christian faith does not tend to extend to matters of ethical concern, in the way that it does for some of the other Christian groups. This combination of beliefs will affect their voting behavior in a number of ways. Their low scores on the ethics dimension will leave them with little sympathy for social and economic policies that are meant to provide some form of government aid to those who do not seem to be doing well on their own. Therefore, we can expect them to take conservative stands on such issues as government-sponsored racial integration and economic programs aimed at aiding the poor.

An even more probable consequence of their conservative religious beliefs is the tendency to favor government intervention to enforce their version of social morality. This flows both from the fact that they adhere to a rigid form of morality themselves (orthodoxy) and from their belief that they must bring others to this point of view (evangelism). Institutionalized immorality is seen as the greatest obstacle to winning souls to Christ through evangelism. Therefore, using government power to eliminate it is easily justified. We can expect them to be the most likely to favor attempts by government to regulate moral behavior or to give their particular religious viewpoint a kind of official status.

Opposed to these conservative Protestants, in a number of ways, will be the liberal Protestants. Members of this group tend

TABLE 2.12
Reiigious Beliefs and Their Political Consequences (Predicted)

Religious Beliefs

| | *Belief Dimension* | | |
Denominational Category	*Orthodoxy*	*Ethicalism*	*Evangelism*
Liberal Protestants	low	high	low
Moderate Protestants	medium	medium	medium
Conservative Protestants	high	low	high
Catholics	medium/high	high	very low

Political Consequences

| | *Type of Consequence* | |
Denominational Category	*Moral Issues*	*Social and Economic Issues*
Liberal Protestants	Liberal	Liberal
Moderate Protestants	Moderate	Moderate
Conservative Protestants	Conservative	Conservative
Catholics	Liberal/Moderate	Liberal

to rank low in adherence to orthodox beliefs but put much emphasis on matters of ethical concern. We can expect this emphasis on ethicalism to be reflected in a heightened willingness to back social and economic programs that are intended to aid the needy. In addition, their low orthodoxy and lack of evangelistic outlook will make them the most likely of all the groups to come down on the side of opposition to any form of linkage between church and state or government intervention in the area of social morality.

Sandwiched in between these two groups in terms of all three belief dimensions are the moderate Protestants. Consequently, predictions about their political behavior can be disposed of rather quickly. The moderate Protestants will fall in between the liberal and conservative Protestants on social and economic issues, and on willingness to use government to regulate social morality.[19]

The Catholics present a somewhat more complex picture. Members of this group tend to rank high on ethicalism, medium to high on orthodoxy, and very low on evangelism. This means that on matters of economic and social policy they are likely to be as liberal as the liberal Protestants. Their fairly strong adherence to orthodox beliefs suggests that most Catholics will adhere to a rather conservative or traditional moral outlook. Yet there are factors that prevent this conservative personal morality from being translated into a call for government regulation of social morality. One such factor is the specific historical situation of Catholics in America. Having always been a religious minority and having often been targets of attacks by the more culturally intolerant elements of American society, Catholics have been led to develop a heightened respect for individual religious freedom and the separation of church and state. But a more important factor is the lack of emphasis on evangelism inherent in the Catholic tradition. This is evidenced by the fact that Catholics score even lower than liberal Protestants on both of our measures of evangelism. For these reasons, Catholics will tend to take liberal positions on most of the moral issues of the day.

However, there will be exceptions to this rule. The distinction between personal morality and the concern with ethicalism is not always clear. While Catholics tend to rank as highly as liberal Protestants in the area of ethical concerns, they are much more conservative in their moral outlook. When personal morality and ethicalism seem to run together, we can expect these groups to react quite differently. An example of such an issue is abortion. For most

Catholics abortion involves the murder of a living human being. Because of this moral perspective, abortion is viewed by many of these Catholics as involving more than just personal morality. Rather it is seen as a matter of the gravest ethical concern. Therefore, it is not regarded as simply a moral issue, but as a social issue demanding government intervention on behalf of another helpless minority. Under such circumstances, Catholics will tend to take an interventionist stand.

THE SOCIAL CHARACTERISTICS OF THE DENOMINATIONAL GROUPS

Before moving on to an examination of the voting patterns of our four religious groups, it is critical that we stop and examine the social characteristics of each. It is conceivable that denominational preference is correlated with other key social characteristics such as income or region. If this is the case, a failure to consider these other variables could lead us to erroneous conclusions about the relationship between religion and voting behavior.

There are actually two different possibilities of which we must be aware. In the first case a third variable could result in a spurious correlation between denominational preference and vote. By knowing beforehand what social variables could conceivably result in such a pattern, we can exercise the proper controls and prevent any false conclusions. On the other hand, a third variable could actually act to suppress a real correlation between religion and vote and cause us to err in the opposite direction. Once again, prior knowledge can help us prevent this error.

The social variables we must examine, because of their possible correlation with both voting behavior and denominational preference, include income, education, region, and age. Table 2.13 presents the breakdown of all four religious categories on each of these variables for 1980.

For our purposes, respondents were divided into three broad income categories. The cutoff points of $12,000 and $25,000 were chosen in an attempt to include the maximum number of respondents in each income bracket. What is important is the percentage of each religious group falling in each of the income categories. The findings indicate that the two wealthiest groups are the liberal Protestants and Catholics. These figures lend credence to

TABLE 2.13
Social Characteristics of the Religious Groups in 1980,
Nonblack Voters Only
(in percentages)

	Income		
	Income Category		
		$12,000	$25,000
	Up to	to	and
Denominational Category	$11,999	$24,999	Over
Liberal Protestants	24	36	40
Moderate Protestants	26	39	35
Conservative Protestants	32	36	32
Catholics	23	37	40
n of cases	621		

	Education		
	Educational Category		
	Grade	High	
Denominational Category	School	School	College
Liberal Protestants	6	42	52
Moderate Protestants	7	50	43
Conservative Protestants	18	45	37
Catholics	8	49	43
n of cases	682		

| | Region | |
| | Regional Category | |
Denominational Category	North	South
Liberal Protestants	79	21
Moderate Protestants	73	27
Conservative Protestants	51	49
Catholics	83	17
n of cases	684	

	Age		
	Age Category		
	18	36	56
	thru	thru	thru
Denominational Category	35	55	98
Liberal Protestants	22	34	44
Moderate Protestants	35	29	36
Conservative Protestants	33	36	31
Catholics	36	36	28
n of cases	684		

other studies that indicate that Catholics have made tremendous economic progress since World War II.[20] It is the conservative Protestants who stand out the most, as a result of their relative poverty. Overall, among Protestants there exists a slight correlation between income and denominational preference, with income decreasing as we move from the liberal to the conservative ends of the spectrum. Therefore, when it makes theoretical sense to do so, income will be examined as an alternative explanation for any apparent correlations between religion and vote.

Aside from income, another possible measure of social class is education. In Table 2.13 respondents are divided into categories including those who received no more than a grade school education, those with at least some high school, and those with at least some college. The educational differences among religious groups are a bit more pronounced than the differences in income. The liberal Protestants clearly stand out as the most educated group, with the Catholics and moderate Protestants about tied for second. As with income, the conservative Protestants stand at the bottom of the ladder. This group does contain a large number of respondents with at least some college education. It stands out mainly because it contains twice as many respondents with only a grade school education than any of the other categories. All in all, education is somewhat correlated with the Protestant spectrum, rising as we move from the conservatives to the liberals. Therefore, it must also be considered when it stands as a credible alternative explanation for any findings that indicate a relationship between religious denomination and vote.

The last two variables to be considered are region and age. In terms of region, it is the conservative Protestants who, once again, differ from the rest. They tend to be much more likely than members of other religious groups to live in the South.[21] Consequently, region must be considered as an alternative explanation whenever the conservative Protestants stand apart from the others in their voting behavior. There is some tendency for age to decline as we move from the liberal to the conservative Protestants, with Catholics being younger than any of the Protestant groups. As with all of the other social characteristics, age will be used as a control variable only when it makes theoretical sense to do so.

Although it is not a social variable in the same sense as the others, party identification ranks as a key independent variable that could conceivably be related to religious preference. Therefore, it is worth considering at this point. Party identification is usually conceived of as a long-term force that adds stability to the voting patterns of the mass electorate. In this it is contrasted with such short-term forces as issues and candidate image, which may vary from election to election. We can expect that religion will affect voting behavior through its influence on both long- and short-term factors. To the extent that it influences the formation of partisan identification, religion will exercise a long-term effect on the American electoral system. This sort of long-range influence will be discussed in Chapter 7. For now, we are primarily concerned with the ways that religious beliefs relate to the more volatile influences that affect the voting decision. Isolating these two different types of factors can be accomplished through normal vote analysis, which involves looking at the voting deviations of each group from what we would expect if its members merely voted on the basis of their partisan identifications. This type of analysis requires that we know the partisan breakdown of each religious group for each election year. These breakdowns are presented in Table 2.14.

TABLE 2.14

Religion by Party Identification, 1960-80, Nonblack Voters Only (in percentages)

Denominational Category	Year					
	1960	*1964*	*1968*	*1972*	*1976*	*1980*
Liberal Protestants						
Dem.	30	40	34	25	25	27
Ind.	18	15	30	32	32	34
Rep.	53	45	36	43	43	39
Moderate Protestants						
Dem.	35	43	30	29	28	29
Ind.	22	22	28	31	35	37
Rep.	43	35	42	41	38	34
Conservative Protestants						
Dem.	63	70	48	45	42	46
Ind.	16	11	33	27	30	26
Rep.	21	19	19	28	28	28
Catholics						
Dem.	66	60	53	52	49	44
Ind.	21	22	28	30	32	33
Rep.	13	18	19	17	19	24
n of cases	1,180	880	824	1,252	1,266	682

For the present, it seems sufficient to point out a few basic facts made obvious by Table 2.14. The first is that the major political parties are not equally represented in each religious group. Among Protestants, the percentage of Republicans declines and that of Democrats increases as we move from the liberal end to the conservative end of the spectrum. Catholics tend to be about as Democratic as conservative Protestants. Second, each religious group has undergone a general dealignment over the years, with the percentage of Independents rising significantly from 1960 to 1980. Finally, the pattern of partisan decline has not been the same for each group. Most conspiciously, the Republicans have lost most heavily among liberal Protestants while the Democrats have declined more among the conservatives. There is a strong hint here of religious influences on partisan change. In Chapter 3 these changes in partisan identification will be considered along with changes in actual voting behavior in order to get a clear sense of how much influence religious beliefs have had on each of the six elections in this most recent 20-year period.

NOTES

1.   George Gallup, "Religion at Home and Abroad," *Public Opinion 2* (March-May 1979): 38-39.

2.   Ibid.

3.   Ibid.

4.   Rodney Stark and Charles Y. Glock, *American Piety: The Nature of Religious Commitment* (Berkeley: University of California Press, 1968).

5.   Ibid., Chapters 2 and 3.

6.   Ibid, pp. 25-32.

7.   Ibid.

8.   Ibid., pp. 32-33.

9.   Ibid., pp. 35-36.

10.   Ibid., pp. 35-39.

11.   Ibid., pp. 58-60.

12.   Ibid., pp. 69-75.

13.   Ibid., pp. 73-75.

14.   Ibid., pp. 75-76.

15.   There are of course other smaller denominations included in our national samples that were not included in the Stark and Glock study. Where possible, such minor denominations were assigned to one or another category on the basis of information provided in Frank S. Mead, *Handbook of Denominations in the United States* (New York: Abingdon Press, 1965). For the exact category assignments see the Appendix at the end of this book.

16.   The vast majority of unclassified Protestants fell into this category because they failed to mention a specific denominational affiliation. The rest

belonged to very small denominations that could not be classified, due to a lack of information about their belief patterns. The "no stated preference" category consists mostly of respondents who stated that they had no religious preference. A few self-described agnostics and atheists were also included.

17. In actuality there are small denominations included in these categories that were not considered by Stark and Glock. However, the number of respondents from these denominations is very small. Therefore, they should have little bearing on the findings.

18. The categorization of denominations from the Gallup survey is not exactly the same as it is for the Michigan surveys. This is due to the differences in the ways that the two polling organizations coded responses to their religious preference question. The two categorization schemes are shown in the Appendix at the end of this book. For the purposes of this analysis, the differences should be of no real significance.

19. Actually, this would be true only for those moderate Protestants who truly fall in the middle of the spectrum on each of the three belief dimensions. In reality the moderate Protestant category will contain a mixture of individuals who fall at different points on the three dimensions. Since this religious category is less pure than the other three it is not a very good predictor of the religious beliefs of individuals who fall within it. For this reason the moderate Protestant category will be deemphasized throughout the rest of our analysis.

20. For a summary of these findings see Wade Clark Roof, "Socioeconomic Differentials Among White Socioreligious Groups in the United States," *Social Forces*, September 1979, pp. 280-89.

21. The South includes the 11 states of the Confederacy (Alabama, Arkansas, Georgia, Florida, Louisiana, Mississippi, North Carolina, South Carolina, Tennessee, Texas, Virginia). The North includes all other states.

3

Religious Beliefs
and Voting Behavior

INTRODUCTION

It has often been said that the central act of representative democracy is voting. In theory, voting is the link that binds governmental elites with those great masses of citizens who fall under their authority. In order to achieve office, an aspiring politician must find some way to put together an electoral coalition large enough to allow him to take his turn at the reins of power. For the average citizen, voting is a way to select those individuals who will rule over them and to cast periodic judgments on these same individuals once they have achieved power. The theoretical end result of all this is the creation of a system in which the policies made by government officials are never too far out of line with the collective will of those that they govern.

In order to understand how closely these theoretical notions resemble reality, it is important that we start by uncovering the factors that result in particular voting decisions. Only by first achieving this can we begin to determine the exact nature of the role that elections play as social devices that link political elites and masses. Much of modern political science has been devoted to understanding these correlates of the voting decision. In this chapter we will focus on one such possible factor: religious beliefs. Our specific goal is to determine if religious beliefs played a role in the outcomes of any of the six most recent presidential elections.

The chapter will be divided into two sections. In the first part we will utilize a standard group voting analysis to show that religious beliefs do seem to have affected the partisan decisions of many voters. In the second part we will add credibility to these findings by ruling out a series of alternative explanations for the relationships found in the first part.

THE VOTING PICTURE: 1960-80

Religion and the Normal Vote

As mentioned in Chapter 2, religious beliefs can be expected to exert both long-term and short-term effects on the presidential voting decision. As a long-term force religion can play a part in the formation of the partisan identifications of individual voters in the mass electorate. In this way religious conflicts can become built into the electoral system, able to exert an indirect effect on the voting decision long after the specific issues of conflict have drifted into the distant past. However, our present concern is with potential short-term religious effects and the ways that these effects can vary from one election to the next. Such a focus will require that we find a way to separate these long- and short-term effects from one another.

Fortunately, the technique of normal vote analysis is ideally suited for our purposes. It simply involves the measurement of deviation from the "normal vote." The normal vote is the percentage vote for each party that we would expect to occur if all voters cast their ballots solely on the basis of their partisan identifications. These partisan identifications are, of course, dependent on the long-term historical experiences of the society under study. The deviations from this normal vote represent the estimate of the short-term forces at work in a given election that cause individuals to vote against the party with which they identify.

Such analysis requires that we know the breakdown of partisan identification by religious denomination. This partisan breakdown was reported in Table 2.14. In normal vote analysis we can assume that Independents divide their votes randomly between the major political parties. This is because the short-term forces at work in the election are assumed to counterbalance each other exactly. With these assumptions in mind, we can estimate the normal vote for each of the six presidential elections. The results are reported in Table 3.1.[1]

The findings of Table 3.1 make it obvious why it would be misleading for us to consider the presidential voting patterns of our four religious groups without considering their underlying partisan distributions. In each year there are vast differences among these groups in the tendency of their members to identify with one or another of the major parties. As of 1960, Democratic strength was to be found mainly among Catholics and conservative Protestants. Republican strength, on the other hand, was centered among the moderate Protestants and even more so among their liberal counterparts. By 1980 the four groups had become much more alike, with the Democrats gaining strength among liberal Protestants while the Republicans gained heavily among both Catholics and conservative Protestants.

A few things need to be said about these general findings. In the first place, while partisan identification can properly be seen as a stabilizing long-term political force, it is not completely immune to the short-term forces affecting specific presidential elections. Second, the nature of the partisan change that has occurred in these 20 years hints strongly at a religious effect. While all of the groups

TABLE 3.1
Normal Vote by Religion, 1960-80
(in percentages)

	Year					
Denominational Category	*1960*	*1964*	*1968*	*1972*	*1976*	*1980*
Liberal Protestants						
Dem.	38	47	49	41	41	44
Rep.	62	53	51	59	59	56
Moderate Protestants						
Dem.	46	54	44	44	45	47
Rep.	54	46	56	56	55	53
Conservative Protestants						
Dem.	71	76	64	59	57	59
Rep.	29	24	36	41	43	41
Catholics						
Dem.	77	71	67	67	65	60
Rep.	23	29	33	33	35	40
n of cases	1,180	880	824	1,252	1,266	682

Source: All of the tables in this chapter were compiled by the author.

have undergone a general dealignment, the rise in the number of Independents has occurred in very different ways. Tables 2.14 and 3.1 show that among liberal Protestants the Democrats have lost only 3 percentage points between 1960 and 1980, while the Republicans have lost 14 points. Among conservative Protestants the Democratic loss has been a full 17 points, while the Republicans have actually gained 7 points. A similar relative Republican gain has occurred among Catholics. However, there is an important difference between Catholics and Protestants in the timing of these changes. Among the Protestant groups the key changes seem to have occurred between 1964 and 1972, while for the Catholics change has been more continuous over all of the years. Different processes, each of which is somehow related to religious beliefs, seem to have been at work.

Thus, while partisan identification can be viewed as a long-term political force, its systematic change from election to election offers us some preliminary evidence of the presence of short-term forces that are somehow connected to religious beliefs. While more will be said about religion and partisan identification in Chapter 7, we will now move on to our main concern: the effect of religious beliefs on the actual presidential vote.

Religion and the Presidential Vote

In Chapter 2 we were able to show that members of our four denominational categories differ widely from one another in terms of three separate dimensions of religious belief. If these beliefs are somehow related to the presidential voting decision, we ought to be able to find very different voting patterns across the religious groups. Such evidence can in fact be found in Table 3.2, which displays the vote breakdown by denominational group for each presidential election from 1960 through 1980.[2]

In each of these elections there were wide disparities among the groups in the way that they voted. In 1960 John Kennedy's strength among Catholics was overwhelming, while conservative Protestants split about evenly between Kennedy and Nixon. On the other hand, roughly seven out of ten liberal and moderate Protestants backed the Republican candidacy of Richard Nixon. In 1964 Lyndon Johnson did better than his predecessor among all three Protestant groups, but not quite as well as Kennedy among Catholics. Overall, the differences across groups were not as sharp

TABLE 3.2
Vote by Religion, 1960-80
(in percentages)

Denominational Category	Candidate		

1960

	Kennedy	Nixon
Liberal Protestants	28	72
Moderate Protestants	32	68
Conservative Protestants	48	52
Catholics	83	17
n of cases	1,198	

1964

	Johnson	Goldwater
Liberal Protestants	51	49
Moderate Protestants	58	42
Conservative Protestants	67	33
Catholics	78	22
n of cases	883	

1968

	Humphrey	Nixon	Wallace
Liberal Protestants	28	64	8
Moderate Protestants	26	64	10
Conservative Protestants	22	46	32
Catholics	54	38	8
n of cases	825		

1972

	McGovern	Nixon
Liberal Protestants	26	74
Moderate Protestants	24	76
Conservative Protestants	20	80
Catholics	38	62
n of cases	1,258	

1976

	Carter	Ford
Liberal Protestants	36	64
Moderate Protestants	40	60
Conservative Protestants	50	50
Catholics	56	44
n of cases	1,271	

1980

	Carter	Reagan	Anderson
Liberal Protestants	32	62	6
Moderate Protestants	26	65	9
Conservative Protestants	40	56	4
Catholics	39	51	9
n of cases	684		

as they had been in 1960, but the Johnson coalition was still disproportionately composed of Catholics and, to a lesser extent, conservative Protestants. The most significant fact about 1968 was the overwhelming desertion of the Democratic candidate by the conservative Protestants. This was largely due to the impressive third-party vote for George Wallace, which was concentrated very heavily among this latter religious category.

In 1972 George McGovern did badly among all groups. Nevertheless, the most impressive success of the Nixon candidacy was its ability to win over a majority of Catholics and an overwhelming majority of conservative Protestants. In the Democratic victories of 1960 and 1964, these two groups had constituted the core of Democratic support. Jimmy Carter's victory in 1976 can largely be attributed to his success in bringing many errant members of these two religious categories back into the Democratic fold. Finally, the voting differences among the four groups declined in the 1980 presidential election. Even with John Anderson pulling away votes from the two major parties, Ronald Reagan was able to win a majority of each of the major religious divisions.

However, this brief summary of the differences in voting patterns among religious groups over the six most recent elections can give us a rather incomplete picture unless we consider group deviations from the normal vote. In order to be able to measure the short-term effect of religion on the various election outcomes, we must go back and consider the partisan breakdowns of the four groups, which were revealed in Table 3.1.

Table 3.3 displays the two-party vote by religious category, once we have eliminated the third-party candidacies of George Wallace and John Anderson. The figures in the last column reveal the deviation of the actual vote from the expected or normal vote for each religious category. When the percentage is preceded by a plus sign it means that the group is voting more Democratic than we would expect. A minus sign indicates deviation in the Republican direction. Finally, Table 3.4 indicates the percentage change in presidential vote for each religious group from one election to the next. Once again, a plus sign represents change in the direction of the Democrats while a minus sign represents change in the opposite direction. Considering all of these tables at once allows us to undertake a more thorough analysis of the effect of religious beliefs on the outcomes of the six elections.

TABLE 3.3

Two-Party Vote and Deviation from the Normal Vote, 1960-80 (in percentages)

Denominational Category	Candidate		
	1960		
	Dem.	*Rep.*	*Dev.*[a]
Liberal Protestants	28	72	−10
Moderate Protestants	32	68	−14
Conservative Protestants	48	52	−23
Catholics	83	17	+6
n of cases	1,198		
	1964		
Liberal Protestants	51	49	+4
Moderate Protestants	58	42	+4
Conservative Protestants	67	33	−9
Catholics	78	22	+7
n of cases	883		
	1968		
Liberal Protestants	31	69	−16 −21[b]
Moderate Protestants	28	72	−15 −18[b]
Conservative Protestants	32	68	−28 −42[b]
Catholics	59	41	−8 −13[b]
n of cases	721		
	1972		
Liberal Protestants	26	74	−15
Moderate Protestants	24	76	−20
Conservative Protestants	20	80	−39
Catholics	38	62	−29
n of cases	1,258		
	1976		
Liberal Protestants	36	64	−5
Moderate Protestants	40	60	−5
Conservative Protestants	50	50	−7
Catholics	56	44	−9
n of cases	1,271		
	1980		
Liberal Protestants	34	66	−9
Moderate Protestants	29	71	−18
Conservative Protestants	42	58	−17
Catholics	43	57	−18
n of cases	634		

[a]This figure is the deviation from the normal vote, the percentage vote that we would expect to find if all partisans voted only on the basis of their party identifications and Independents split evenly between the two major parties.

[b]This second figure is the deviation from the normal Democratic vote for each group if we count both Nixon and Wallace voters as anti-Democratic votes.

When John Kennedy began his drive for the Democratic presidential nomination in 1960, he had to overcome the fears that many Democratic party leaders had about the effect of his Catholicism on the vote. These fears grew out of the knowledge that the national Democratic majority was built largely around two major religious groups, Catholics and conservative Protestants. This coalition had been possible as long as elections were fought primarily along the lines of the New Deal issues, which were rooted heavily in economic class conflict. As of the 1930s, these two religious groups accounted for a disproportionately large percentage of the white lower classes. What the Democratic strategists feared in 1960 was the emergence of a new and cross-cutting issue based on Kennedy's religious affiliation. There was good reason to suspect that a great many conservative Protestants would be sufficiently turned off by this Catholicism issue to cast their ballots for his Republican opponent. As mentioned in Chapter 1, conflict between these pietistically oriented conservative Protestants and the liturgically oriented Catholics extended as far back as the early nineteenth century.

TABLE 3.4
Vote Change by Religion, 1956-80

	Year					
Denominational Category	*1956-1960*	*1960-1964*	*1964-1968*	*1968-1972*	*1972-1976*	*1976-1980*
Liberal Protestants	−1	+23	−20 −23*	−5	+10	−2
Moderate Protestants	+2	+26	−30 −32*	−4	+16	−11
Conservative Protestants	−2	+19	−35 −45*	−12	+30	−8
Catholics	+39	−5	−19 −24*	−21	+18	−13

*This second percentage for 1968 includes the Wallace vote as a Democratic loss. All other percentages are based only on the two-party vote. Ignoring the Wallace vote greatly understates the religion effect since Wallace's support came overwhelmingly from conservative Protestants.

+ indicates change in the direction of the Democrats.

− indicates change in the direction of the Republicans.

The figures in Table 3.3 suggest that this religious conflict did affect the outcome of the 1960 election. Catholics voted more Democratic than we would have expected, while all of the Protestant groups deviated from the normal vote in the Republican direction. In keeping with the above-mentioned expectations based on the history of American religious conflict, the conservative Protestants were by far the most likely to desert the Democratic party. It seems that religious conflict did in fact play an important role in the partisan decisions of many voters. Table 3.4 can give us added insight into the effect of the Kennedy nomination regarding this religious conflict. In 1956 Adlai Stevenson had done very poorly among both Catholics and conservative Protestants. The Kennedy candidacy managed to pull a huge percentage of Catholics back into the Democratic fold. The conservative Protestants, evidently turned off by Kennedy, not only failed to return but actually moved a little further away from their traditional party. This fact almost did in the Kennedy candidacy and left him in a position of great political insecurity once it came time to assume the presidency.

The assassination of President Kennedy and the nomination of Lyndon Johnson by the Democratic party effectively removed the Catholicism issue from the 1964 election. The overall short-term political forces present in this particular year were, of course, much more pro-Democratic than they had been in 1960, resulting in the Johnson landslide. This pro-Democratic slant is evident in Table 3.3, which shows that three out of the four major religious groups deviated from the normal vote in the Democratic direction. The one exception is the conservative Protestants who deviated by 9 points in the Republican direction. All in all there is some slight evidence of a religious effect, with a full 16 points separating the deviation of the conservative Protestants from that of the Catholics. This religious effect is actually somewhat distorted by the normal vote analysis because it ignores the changes in group party identification that occurred between 1960 and 1964. When these changes in partisan identification are considered, the overall difference between the liberal and conservative Protestants increases, because the liberals were becoming somewhat more Democratic relative to the conservatives than they had been in 1960. On the other hand the difference between conservative Protestants and Catholics actually declines, due to the six-point drop in the expected Democratic vote among Catholics, which probably occurred as a result of the loss of the Catholic candidate.

In general two things can be said about the impact of religious beliefs on the 1964 election. In the first place, while such an impact seems to have been present it was clearly weaker than it had been in 1960. Second, the nature of this religious impact seems to have been different from that of four years earlier. In 1960 the main polarization had been between Catholics and Protestants, and in particular between Catholics and conservative Protestants. In 1964 the split between the latter two groups continued but with a greatly decreased intensity. On the other hand the gap between liberal and conservative Protestants widened somewhat, as the Democrats gained slightly among the liberals relative to the conservatives. (This polarization of the Protestant groups in terms of the religion factor actually drove them closer together in the overall vote, since the liberals had long been much more Republican than the conservatives.)

The findings for the 1968 election seem to indicate a tremendous intensification of the religious effect found in 1964.[3] In terms of the two-party vote the overall short-term forces worked heavily in favor of the Republicans, with all four religious groups deviating from the normal vote in the Republican direction. Still the differences among the groups are quite impressive. The polarization between Catholics and conservative Protestants in terms of their support for the Democratic candidate increased sharply, reaching the level that had existed in 1960. Considering the overall trends in the election, Hubert Humphrey managed to hold his ground rather well among Catholic voters. If he had succeeded in holding onto Democratic partisans from the other three religious categories as well as he had among Catholics, he would have certainly emerged victorious. However, such was not to be the case. Humphrey's biggest electoral failure occurred among the conservative Protestants. Members of this group registered their displeasure with the Democratic party in a number of ways. In the first place the percentage of conservative Protestants identifying with the Democratic party dropped a full 22 points in the four years from 1964 to 1968. But even among those who maintained their Democratic affiliation the rates of electoral defection were astounding. If just the two-party vote is considered, the conservative Protestants voted 28 points less Democratic than we would have expected on the basis of party identification alone. Even this does not tell the whole story. An incredible 32 percent of all conservative Protestants cast their ballots in favor of the third-party candidacy of George

Wallace. If we consider both Nixon and Wallace votes together as anti-Democratic votes, the deviation of this group from their expected Democratic vote was an astounding 42 percentage points.[4]

This tremendous loss of support by the Democratic party among conservative Protestants greatly widened the electoral gap between this particular Protestant group and the Catholics. The result was a shattering of the basic New Deal Democratic coalition that had rested in large part on these two groups. Moreover, something else seemed to be happening in 1968. This was the further polarization of liberal and conservative Protestants regarding the way they seemed to be reacting to the political forces at large in the 1960s. This polarization had been hinted at in 1964, but 1968 saw a massive increase in its magnitude. Not surprisingly, the overall short-term forces at work in the 1968 presidential election pushed both groups more into the Republican camp than they had been in 1964; but the rates of change were very different for the two Protestant groups. As Table 3.4 shows, the liberal Protestants voted 23 points less Democratic than they had in 1964, while the figure for the conservatives was 45 percent. The net effect of all this was that Hubert Humphrey pulled down a lower percentage of votes among the conservatives than among the liberals; this is in spite of the fact that only eight years earlier normal vote analysis would have predicted a Democratic vote among the former group 33 points higher than among the latter. It seems clear that political forces, somehow related to religious beliefs, were at work here.

The religious conflicts inherent in the three-way battle of 1968 became ever more intensified by 1972. The overall short-term forces at work in this latter election were even more slanted in the direction of the Republican candidate than they had been four years earlier, resulting in a massive landslide victory for Richard Nixon. Nevertheless, within this conglomeration of political forces the impact of differences in religious beliefs among the four groups is readily apparent. This impact was not reflected in changes in party identification, as the Republicans made significant gains among each of the Protestant groups. This fact probably reflected the overall magnitude of the short-term Republican advantage. However, a powerful religious effect is made glaringly obvious by the varying rates of deviation from the normal vote, shown in Table 3.3. The polarization of the liberal and conservative Protestants, which had begun at least by 1964 and had greatly increased in 1968, continued in full swing. While the liberals deviated by 15 points in the

Republican direction, Democratic defections among the conservatives amounted to more than 2.5 times that figure. There is reason to believe that the conservative Protestants' disenchantment with George McGovern closely resembled their disenchantment with Hubert Humphrey four years earlier. The Democratic vote among this group was only 2 points lower in 1972 than it had been in 1968. The difference in conservative support for Richard Nixon in these two years may have been due to the absence of the Wallace candidacy in 1972. This possibility will be examined more closely in Chapter 5, when we consider the relationship between religious beliefs and a variety of political issues. Whatever the specific reasons, the net result was that in 1972, as in 1968, the Democratic candidate actually ended up getting a lower percentage of votes among the conservative Protestants than among the liberals.

While the religious effect among Protestants in 1972 showed a great consistency with 1968, its effect on Catholics could hardly have been more different. While Humphrey had managed to pull down 54 percent of the three-way vote, the figure for McGovern dropped to 38 percent. As Table 3.4 indicates, it was among this group that the Democrats suffered their biggest losses between the two election years. Unlike with the conservative Protestants, this massive loss in Democratic strength among Catholics seems to have been tied into political forces unique to the 1972 election. In 1976 Democratic voting strength among this latter group returned to the majority level it had been at in 1968. All of these facts give us reason to believe that the McGovern candidacy managed to turn off Catholics and conservative Protestants in very different ways. This negative appeal among the two groups that had represented the bulk of the New Deal Democratic coalition insured the most massive Democratic defeat in the history of the modern party system.

While the 1968 and 1972 elections represent distinct examples of how religious beliefs can play a powerful role in presidential voting behavior, 1976 seems to have been a very different kind of electoral event. In this year the overall Republican advantage in the short-term political forces at work in the election was not large enough to overcome the Democratic edge in party identification. The figures in Table 3.3 indicate that group differences in religious beliefs seem to have played little or no role in the election outcome. The differences among all four religious groups, in terms of their deviation from the normal vote, amounted to a meager 4 percent.

Table 3.4 gives us a clue as to how Jimmy Carter managed to pull off his electoral victory. While Carter managed to do much better than George McGovern among each of the groups, his biggest gains occurred among the two most important segments of the old New Deal coalition, the Catholics and the conservative Protestants. The gains made among the latter group are particularly impressive, for they represented a clear break with a political trend that had begun by 1964. Undoubtedly, some of this success was due to the tremendous publicity given to Carter's own fundamentalist Christian beliefs. But whatever the reasons, the decline of religiously based conflicts in 1976 played a large part in the success of the Democrats in reconstructing much of the old majority coalition that had been so badly divided in the two previous presidential elections.

The lack of a significant religious impact on the 1976 race seems to have been largely carried over into 1980. Not surprisingly, each of the four groups moved in the Republican direction, providing the basis for the impressive Reagan victory. But the differences among the religious categories did not come close to approaching the levels of 1968 or 1972. Nevertheless, some small religious effect may be indicated by Table 3.4, which shows that Carter's vote decline from 1976 to 1980 amounted to only 2 percent among liberal Protestants, 8 percent among conservative Protestants, and 13 percent among Catholics. The claims of the moral majority to the contrary, it was the Catholics who stood out the most in their rejection of the Democratic candidate. There is little evidence of a groundswell of evangelical support for Ronald Reagan. Among conservative Protestants, the victorious Reagan pulled down a vote that was still 22 percentage points lower than Richard Nixon had received eight years earlier.

Nevertheless, the controversy surrounding the impact of religious voting on the 1980 presidential election would seem to merit a closer look at this particular contest. The varying interpretations of the election outcome have political as well as academic implications. In the immediate aftermath of the 1980 election, leaders of the religious right argued strenuously that Ronald Reagan owed his victory in large part to the politicization of conservative Christians throughout the United States. If such claims are true, or if they are widely perceived to be true, they could vastly increase the leverage of these religiously oriented conservatives in their attempts to influence the policymaking process. Thus we are faced with a clear-cut example of where academic interpretation of social events has more than a theoretical importance. As could be expected, the debate has begun to stimulate academic research on the role of the religious right in the 1980 presidential race. Most of the resulting articles have questioned the importance of the political activity of the religious right in the impressive victory of Ronald Reagan.[5]

The findings that we have presented thus far should add weight to this majority opinion. This case can be further strengthened by the findings of Tables 3.5 and 3.6, which provide the breakdown of the presidential vote for 1972 and 1980 by religious group while controlling for party identification. These tables enable us to take a somewhat more detailed look at the information provided by the deviations from the normal vote shown in Table 3.3. The two years were chosen so that we could compare 1980 with a year in which the religious impact on the presidential vote was at its highest point.

TABLE 3.5
Religion by Vote by Party Identification, 1972
(in percentages)

	Candidate	
Denominational Category	*McGovern*	*Nixon*
Democrats		
Liberal Protestants	53	47
Moderate Protestants	50	50
Conservative Protestants	33	67
Catholics	53	47
n of cases	230	247
Independents		
Liberal Protestants	34	66
Moderate Protestants	27	73
Conservative Protestants	14	86
Catholics	30	70
n of cases	105	273
Republicans		
Liberal Protestants	6	94
Moderate Protestants	4	96
Conservative Protestants	3	97
Catholics	9	91
n of cases	21	376

TABLE 3.6
Religion by Vote by Party Identification, 1980
(in percentages)

Denominational Category	Candidate	
	Carter	*Reagan*
Democrats		
Liberal Protestants	74	26
Moderate Protestants	62	38
Conservative Protestants	75	25
Catholics	69	31
n of cases	165	72
Independents		
Liberal Protestants	37	63
Moderate Protestants	27	73
Conservative Protestants	24	76
Catholics	34	66
n of cases	61	137
Republicans		
Liberal Protestants	5	95
Moderate Protestants	3	97
Conservative Protestants	3	97
Catholics	7	93
n of cases	9	190

In 1972 large differences appeared between liberal and conservative Protestants in their support of the Democratic candidate. Among both Democrats and Independents the liberals were 20 percentage points more supportive of George McGovern than the conservatives. Among Republicans the virtual unanimous support of Richard Nixon prevented the emergence of significant differences among the religious groups. In contrast the voting differences among religious groups in 1980 were much more modest. Among Democrats the two major Protestant groups were virtually identical in their support of Jimmy Carter, while Catholics were not far behind. Some religious effect does seem to have been present among Independents, with liberal Protestants being 13 percent more supportive of the Democratic candidate than the conservative Protestants. Still, these figures seem to add further credibility to the argument that the overall impact of religion on the 1980 presidential election did not begin to approach that of other recent years such as 1968 and 1972.

Before finishing this section, one final table helps to make our argument complete. Table 3.7 displays summary measures of the overall long- and short-term impact of religious denomination on the presidential elections of 1960 through 1980. This type of measure was developed to separate the long- and short-term impact on voting behavior of an independent variable such as religion.[6] The larger the long-term measure L, the stronger the relationship between religion and the normal or expected vote. The larger the short-term measure S, the stronger the relationship between religion and the deviation from that normal vote. The short-term measure is of special interest to our present discussion. The figures in Table 3.7 confirm our claim that the largest religious impact occurred in the presidential elections of 1960, 1968, and 1972. Only in 1976 did religion have less of an impact than it did in 1980. The short-term figure for 1980 was only 40 percent of what it had been in 1972. Thus while some increase in the influence of religion on presidential voting behavior did seem to occur between 1976 and 1980, a general overview of the last two decades does not lead to the conclusion that Ronald Reagan more than other recent presidents owes his election to the efforts of certain religious groups over those of others.

TABLE 3.7
Summary of Religion Effect, 1960-80

Year	L (long-term)	S (short-term)
1960	15.892	7.352
1964	10.918	3.464
1968[a]	9.773	6.749
1972	10.749	7.334
1976	9.297	1.624
1980[b]	7.491	2.915

[a]Includes Wallace voters. Nixon and Wallace voters are added together. Wallace voters are included in calculating expected vote.

[b]Excludes Anderson voters from calculations of both expected and actual vote.

In summary, the largest religious impact on presidential voting seems to have occurred in 1960, 1968, and 1972. At this point we do not know exactly how religious beliefs managed to affect the outcomes of these three elections. Later on we will attempt to determine the exact mechanisms that led to the strong relationship between denominational category and presidential vote that we found in these years. But the evidence presented thus far does provide us with certain clues that could aid in our search. In 1960, for instance, the inflated Catholic vote for Kennedy and his relatively weak showing among conservative Protestants give us reason to suspect that the Catholicism issue was indeed a key factor that influenced the partisan decisions of many voters. The data also seem to indicate a growing polarization of the liberal and conservative Protestants beginning in 1964 and peaking in 1968 and 1972. This suggests the development of new issues, somehow based on religious beliefs, which cut across this particular series of elections. On the other hand, the extraordinarily negative response of Catholics to the McGovern candidacy seems to have been based on factors unique to the 1972 election. Each of these clues will be considered when we begin our analysis of how religious beliefs relate to issue stands in Chapter 5.

THE SOCIAL CORRELATES OF RELIGION

The data examined thus far seem to offer strong evidence that religious beliefs have played a major role in determining the outcomes of a number of recent presidential elections, particularly those of 1960, 1968, and 1972. In order to add credibility to this conclusion, it is important that we take time to rule out possible alternative explanations for the apparent relationships that we have reported. It is theoretically possible that other social variables could be correlated with both religious denomination and presidential vote. These possible confounding variables include region, income, education, and age. Each must be controlled for if erroneous conclusions about the relationship between religious beliefs and presidential voting are to be prevented.

Religion and Region

Probably the most serious threat to the conclusions reached thus far from our analysis of the presidential voting patterns of the four major religious groups involves the region variable. Much has been made in the literature on American electoral behavior about the unique political tendencies of those who live in the 11 states of the South. While Southerners have until fairly recently been overwhelmingly Democratic in terms of party affiliation, their relatively conservative stands on a number of political issues have often left them at odds with majority tendencies within the national Democratic party. It is usually assumed that it is this basic tension between party affiliation and issue positions that accounts for the strong tendency for Southern Democrats in the last few decades to break party ranks and vote for Republican presidential candidates. Therefore, region has emerged as a major explanatory variable to be taken into account in any thorough analysis of presidential voting behavior.

The significance of all this for our own study stems from the fact that members of the four religious groups are not equally distributed between the North and South. As pointed out in Chapter 2, the conservative Protestants are far more likely than members of the other three religious groups to live in the South. This presents us with the possibility that any unique voting behavior displayed by conservative Protestants may actually be a function of region rather than of religious beliefs. In particular the disproportionately large percentage of Southerners found among the conservative Protestants may actually explain the fact that this religious group deviated from the normal vote much more in the Republican direction than any of the other religious groups, in each of the three presidential elections in which the religious effect seemed strongest.

In order to test for this possibility, Table 3.8 displays the voting patterns of each religious group in each of the three years, controlling for region of residence. The findings for the 1972 election are the most clear-cut. In this case both religion and region seem to have exercised powerful effects on voting behavior. The regional effect is made obvious by the fact that for each religious group Southerners deviated much more in the Republican direction than did Northerners. On the other hand the powerful religious effect, found in the nation as a whole, holds up very well in each of the two regions. Whereas the difference between liberal and conservative Protestants in their rates of deviation was 24 points in the country as a whole, it registered at 19 points in the North and 18 points in the South. Less surprisingly, the strong tendency for Catholics to reject the candidacy of George McGovern also

TABLE 3.8

Religion by Vote by Region, 1972, 1968, 1960

(in percentages)

Denominational Category	Candidate		
	1972		
	North		
	McGovern	*Nixon*	*Dev.*
Liberal Protestants	27	73	−10
Moderate Protestants	26	74	−16
Conservative Protestants	21	79	−29
Catholics	40	60	−26
n of cases	305	691	
	South		
Liberal Protestants	25	75	−31
Moderate Protestants	15	85	−39
Conservative Protestants	18	82	−49
Catholics	22	78	−57
n of cases	51	211	
	1968		
	North		
	Humphrey	*Nixon*	*Wallace*	*Dev.[a]*
Liberal Protestants	28	65	7	−16
Moderate Protestants[b]	26	65	9	−17
Conservative Protestants	26	65	9	−23
Catholics[b]	55	39	6	−12
n of cases	237	366	50	
	South		
Liberal Protestants	27	60	13	−32
Moderate Protestants	19	62	19	−35
Conservative Protestants	20	37	43	−52
Catholics	42	25	33	−33
n of cases	40	78	54	
	1960		
	North		
	Kennedy	*Nixon*	*Dev.*
Liberal Protestants	20	80	−8
Moderate Protestants	32	68	−15
Conservative Protestants	38	62	−1
Catholics	84	16	+7
n of cases	421	510	
	South		
Liberal Protestants	48	52	−19
Moderate Protestants[b]	30	70	−3
Conservative Protestants	52	48	−31
Catholics[b]	74	26	+2
n of cases	136	131	

[a]This figure is the deviation from the normal Democratic vote for each group if we count both Nixon and Wallace votes as anti-Democratic votes. The other deviations are based only on the two-party vote.

[b]Less than 30 cases in this category. This makes the percentages highly unstable.

holds up when controls for region are instituted. For the nation as a whole the Catholics were 14 points more likely than the liberal Protestants to deviate in the Republican direction. In the North this figure was 16 points, while in the South it was a full 26 points. It is clear that in the case of the 1972 election, region does not explain away the strong relationship between religion and presidential voting found in Table. 3.3.

For the 1960 and 1968 elections the findings are a bit more complex. Whereas in 1972 region and religion seem to have exercised strong independent effects on the presidential vote, in these other two elections their effects seem to have been more interactive in nature. In 1960 the main line of religious polarization was between Catholics and conservative Protestants. Whereas Catholics deviated from the normal vote by 6 points in the Democratic direction, the conservative Protestants did so by 23 points in the opposite direction. When region is controlled for, this polarization is substantially reduced in the North but not in the South. Taking the North alone causes the difference to drop to 8 points. While still significant this figure is considerably less than the 29-point difference found in the nation as a whole. In the South the difference actually grows to 33 points.[7] These figures suggest the occurrence of an interactive effect between religion and region. While each of these two variables seems to have exerted a substantial impact on the vote, the combination of being both a conservative Protestant and living in the South increased the tendency to desert the Democratic party to a level we would not have expected from each of the two variables taken separately.

These conclusions also seem to apply to the 1968 election. In this case substantial polarization occurred both between liberal and conservative Protestants on the one hand, and between Catholics and conservative Protestants on the other. When region is controlled for, the gap between liberal and conservative Protestants in their percent deviation drops from 21 points in the nation as a whole to 7 points in the North taken alone. In a similar fashion the gap between Catholics and conservative Protestants drops from 29 points in the nation as a whole to 11 points in the North alone. While these figures are still significant they show that the religious impact was not nearly as strong in the North as it was in the South, where the differences remain at 20 points between the liberal and conservative Protestants and 19 points between conservative

Protestants and Catholics. Once again, an interactive effect between religion and region seems to have been present.

The findings presented thus far suggest that while region is a variable of substantial importance in affecting the vote, it cannot explain away the powerful relationships found between voting behavior and religious belief. In the 1972 election religion seemed to exercise a powerful effect on voting behavior in both regions of the country. In 1960 and 1968 religion seemed to exercise a powerful impact on the vote in the South and a less powerful but still substantial impact in the North. Still, skeptics might argue that we are measuring region in the wrong sort of way. It might be argued that what is really important is not where a respondent lived at the time of the election but rather where he actually grew up. The differences between the political environments of someone growing up in the North and someone growing up in the South may leave their impact on the political orientations of these individuals long after they have moved to a different region of the country.

Fortunately, this type of counterhypothesis can easily be tested. Table 3.9 displays the voting patterns of members of the four religious groups for 1972, controlling for the region of the country in which they grew up. It can quickly be seen that the figures are

TABLE 3.9
Religion by Vote by Region of Birth, 1972
(in percentages)

Denominational Category	Candidate		
	McGovern	*Nixon*	*Dev.*
	North		
Liberal Protestants	26	74	−10
Moderate Protestants	25	75	−16
Conservative Protestants	22	78	−28
Catholics	39	61	−27
n of cases	282	671	
	South		
Liberal Protestants	29	71	−38
Moderate Protestants	22	78	−36
Conservative Protestants	18	82	−51
Catholics	26	74	−59
n of cases	54	190	

almost identical to those in Table 3.8. Wide gaps between liberal and conservative Protestants in their rates of deviation from the normal vote persist in both regions, although they are slightly reduced for the South. The findings concerning the unpopularity of McGovern among Catholics also remain unaltered.

Table 3.5 added further credibility to our findings by displaying the voting patterns of each religious group in 1972, controlling for party identification. As a final test this procedure is repeated in Table 3.10 for the North alone. (Such complex controls were not feasible for the South because of the small number of cases in each subcategory.) In both tables wide gaps appear among religious groups in their support for the Democratic candidate.

TABLE 3.10
Religion by Vote by Party Identification, 1972
(Excluding the South)
(in percentages)

	Candidate	
Denominational Category	*McGovern*	*Nixon*
Democrats		
Liberal Protestants	58	42
Moderate Protestants	58	42
Conservative Protestants	40	60
Catholics	56	44
n of cases	189	154
Independents		
Liberal Protestants	38	62
Moderate Protestants	28	72
Conservative Protestants	19	81
Catholics	32	68
n of cases	97	216
Republicans		
Liberal Protestants	5	95
Moderate Protestants	5	95
Conservative Protestants	5	95
Catholics	9	91
n of cases	19	317

Among both Democrats and Independents, liberal Protestants were much more likely than conservatives to vote Democratic. Among Republicans these religious group differences were prevented because of the near unanimous support of all the groups for the candidacy of Richard Nixon. Within each of the party groups, support for McGovern among Catholics and liberal Protestants was very nearly equal. Thus the difference between these two groups in their deviation from the normal vote was primarily a result of the fact that Catholics were so much more likely than liberal Protestants to identify with the Democratic party. But the most important finding here is that the trends in party desertion among religious groups found in the nation as a whole were not a result of the regional distinctiveness of the South. Clearly the differences in the regional distributions of our four religious groups do not explain away the apparent impact of religious beliefs on presidential voting behavior.

Religion and the Other Social Variables

There is little reason to suspect that the other social variables—income, education, and age—can explain away the relationships we have found between religious belief and the presidential vote. Education and income, being measures of social class, can be expected to be positively related to the tendency to vote Republican. Yet, as shown in Chapter 2, both of these measures decline as we move from the liberal to the conservative ends of the Protestant spectrum. Therefore, they would not seem to be capable of explaining the tendency of conservative Protestants to be especially likely to desert the Democratic party in presidential elections. If anything, social class can be seen as a countervailing tendency that tends to offset some of the effect of religious beliefs on the vote. In addition there is no obvious reason to expect that the uneven distribution of the four groups in terms of age can account for the powerful relationships mentioned above.

Nevertheless, in a skeptical world it is always nice to be able to offer empirical validation of one's claims. For this reason Tables 3.11, 3.12, and 3.13 display the relationship between religion and presidential vote, controlling for each of the three social variables.[8] It can be seen that none of these variables explains away the strong relationship we have found between denominational category and

TABLE 3.11
Religion by Vote by Income, 1960, 1968, 1972
(in percentages)

Denominational Category	Candidate			
	1960			
	Less Than $6,000			
	Kennedy	*Nixon*		*Dev.*
Liberal Protestants	31	69		−10
Moderate Protestants	35	65		−14
Conservative Protestants	52	48		−20
Catholics	83	17		+3
n of cases	326	346		
	$6,000 and Over			
Liberal Protestants	23	77		−13
Moderate Protestants	27	73		−16
Conservative Protestants	38	62		−32
Catholics	85	15		+9
n of cases	227	291		
	1968			
	Less Than $8,000			
	Humphrey	*Nixon*	*Wallace*	*Dev.* *
Liberal Protestants	30	58	12	−27
Moderate Protestants	26	64	10	−23
Conservative Protestants	23	42	36	−41
Catholics	52	43	5	−17
n of cases	127	205	57	
	$8,000 and Over			
Liberal Protestants	26	68	6	−17
Moderate Protestants	25	64	11	−15
Conservative Protestants	23	55	23	−44
Catholics	57	34	9	−9
n of cases	146	232	45	
	1972			
	Less than $10,000			
	McGovern	*Nixon*		*Dev.*
Liberal Protestants	26	74		−21
Moderate Protestants	26	74		−20
Conservative Protestants	23	77		−41
Catholics	44	56		−25
n of cases	172	391		
	$10,000 and Over			
Liberal Protestants	27	73		−7
Moderate Protestants	23	77		−21
Conservative Protestants	17	83		−36
Catholics	33	67		−33
n of cases	175	486		

*This figure is the deviation from the normal Democratic vote for each group if we count both Nixon and Wallace votes as anti-Democratic votes.

the tendency to deviate from the normal vote in each of the three years. However, some interesting interactive effects seem to be present.

In each of the three years the religious effect seems to be stronger in the higher income category. In 1960 the polarization between Catholics and conservative Protestants, in terms of their deviation from the normal vote, was especially strong among those who made over $6,000 a year. In 1968 the split between liberal and conservative Protestants was also higher among those in the upper income bracket. The same was true for the split between Catholics and conservative Protestants. In 1972 the polarizations between liberal and conservative Protestants on one hand, and Catholics and liberal Protestants on the other, were much greater among those making over $10,000 than among those earning less than this figure. Whatever the dominant religious polarizations happen to be in a given election, they seem to be more prominent among the well-to-do.

These generalizations regarding the interactive effect between religion and income can also be applied to the relationship between religion and education, in two out of the three years. In both 1960 and 1968 the dominant polarizations mentioned above were considerably stronger among the higher-educated group than among those with less than a high school degree. Only in 1972 did education seem to make little difference. In this case the gap between liberal and conservative Protestants was actually somewhat larger among the less educated, while the split between liberal Protestants and Catholics was the same for both educational groups.

There is no consistency to the way that age affects the relationship between religious belief and the vote. In 1960 the polarization between Catholics and conservative Protestants was especially strong among the young. In 1968 the dominant polarizations were approximately equal for each age cohort. Finally, in 1972 the gaps between liberal and conservative Protestants and between liberal Protestants and Catholics were considerably stronger among those over 40.

So where do we stand at this point? In Chapter 2 we were able to develop a denominational categorization scheme and show that it was a meaningful predictor of three separate dimensions of religious belief. We were also able to show how these religious beliefs might be related to political attitudes and ultimately to presidential voting behavior. In this chapter we have shown that

TABLE 3.12
Religion by Vote by Education, 1960, 1968, 1972
(in percentages)

Denominational Category	Candidate			
1960				
Less Than High School Degree				
	Kennedy	*Nixon*		*Dev.*
Liberal Protestants	30	70		−10
Moderate Protestants	35	65		−18
Conservative Protestants	53	47		−13
Catholics	82	18		+3
n of cases	254	245		
At Least High School Degree				
Liberal Protestants	27	73		−11
Moderate Protestants	30	70		−12
Conservative Protestants	41	59		−37
Catholics	83	17		+8
n of cases	302	396		
1968				
Less Than High School Degree				
	Humphrey	*Nixon*	*Wallace*	*Dev.* *
Liberal Protestants	29	55	16	−29
Moderate Protestants	39	47	14	−22
Conservative Protestants	28	40	33	−40
Catholics	63	31	6	−20
n of cases	104	112	45	
At Least High School Degree				
Liberal Protestants	28	67	6	−18
Moderate Protestants	20	71	9	−17
Conservative Protestants	17	53	31	−44
Catholics	51	41	8	−10
n of cases	173	332	59	
1972				
Less Than High School Degree				
	McGovern	*Nixon*		*Dev.*
Liberal Protestants	28	72		−20
Moderate Protestants	26	74		−29
Conservative Protestants	21	79		−48
Catholics	38	62		−34
n of cases	109	265		
At Least High School Degree				
Liberal Protestants	26	74		−13
Moderate Protestants	23	77		−16
Conservative Protestants	19	81		−34
Catholics	38	62		−27
n of cases	247	636		

*This figure is the deviation from the normal Democratic vote for each group if we count both Nixon and Wallace votes as anti-Democratic votes.

TABLE 3.13
Religion by Vote by Age, 1960, 1968, 1972
(in percentages)

Denominational Category	Candidate			
	1960			
	18 through 40			
	Kennedy	Nixon		Dev.
Liberal Protestants	22	78		−9
Moderate Protestants	35	65		−21
Conservative Protestants	53	47		−26
Catholics	85	15		+11
n of cases	224	233		
	41 and Above			
Liberal Protestants	31	69		−12
Moderate Protestants	30	70		−11
Conservative Protestants	44	56		−22
Catholics	81	19		+3
n of cases	333	408		
	1968			
	18 through 40			
	Humphrey	Nixon	Wallace	Dev.*
Liberal Protestants	31	60	9	−25
Moderate Protestants	28	54	18	−21
Conservative Protestants	12	55	33	−44
Catholics	54	36	10	−13
n of cases	107	152	49	
	41 and Above			
Liberal Protestants	27	65	8	−19
Moderate Protestants	24	70	6	−17
Conservative Protestants	28	42	30	−41
Catholics	54	40	6	−13
n of cases	170	291	55	
	1972			
	18 through 40			
	McGovern	Nixon		Dev.
Liberal Protestants	28	72		−16
Moderate Protestants	29	71		−16
Conservative Protestants	22	78		−33
Catholics	41	59		−26
n of cases	170	363		
	41 and Above			
Liberal Protestants	26	74		−13
Moderate Protestants	21	79		−22
Conservative Protestants	18	82		−44
Catholics	35	65		−33
n of cases	185	535		

*This figure is the deviation from the normal Democratic vote for each group if we count both Nixon and Wallace votes as anti-Democratic votes.

these religious beliefs do in fact have a significant effect on the presidential vote. Other social variables do not seem to be able to explain away this apparent relationship. But indirectly our findings have also suggested something else. The strength of the relationship between religious belief and presidential voting has varied considerably from one election to the next. It seems that four years can make all the difference in the world. More likely, the strength of the religion factor is heavily dependent on the nature of the candidates nominated by the major parties. In Chapter 4 we will attempt to examine this proposition more directly.

NOTES

1.   For the 1960, 1964, and 1968 election studies an error in question wording resulted in the failure to distinguish between Southern Baptists and members of other Baptist groups. This is significant because Southern Baptists represent a key component of our conservative Protestant group, whereas American Baptists fall into our moderate category. In order to adjust for this we have assumed that Baptists residing in the South belong to the Southern Baptist convention, while those residing in the North do not. This means that some respondents will be incorrectly classified. However, this question wording error was corrected by the time of the 1972 election study. We have used this 1972 data to estimate the percent of error for the three previous election years. It turns out that approximately 8 percent of all those we have classified as moderate Protestants are really conservatives, and approximately 11 percent of all those we have classified as conservative Protestants are really moderates. To the extent that this affects our findings, it will bias the results against the hypothesis that religious beliefs influence political behavior. This is because our moderate and conservative categories will seem to be more alike than they are in reality. Thus, any findings that suggest that religious beliefs do in fact have a political impact will be all the more impressive.

2.   A word needs to be said here about the moderate Protestants. Among the liberal and conservative Protestants there is a high degree of consensus on religious beliefs. This is much less true of the moderate category, which contains a far greater degree of variation of belief. For this reason predictions about the political behavior of members of this group will be much shakier than for members of the other groups. Fortunately, this does not present a major problem since evidence that religious beliefs affect political behavior can be arrived at by comparing the other three religious categories.

3.   The reader will immediately wonder if the widening split between the liberal and conservative Protestants had something to do with the rise of the civil rights issue. This idea would not be inconsistent with our overall model. In Chapter 5 we will argue that religious beliefs affect voting behavior by first affecting attitudes toward many political issues of the day. A word should also be said here about exactly what constitutes a significant difference between

groups in terms of deviation from the normal vote. We have avoided using measures of statistical significance because the large number of cases makes it rather easy to achieve. For instance a difference of only 7 percentage points between two religious groups of at least 200 cases each would be statistically significant at the .05 level (using a difference of proportions test). The actual differences found between religious groups in 1960, 1968, and 1972 far exceed this minimum level.

4. The normal vote figures for 1968 were calculated twice: once including Wallace voters and once excluding them. The appropriate figures were then used as a baseline when calculating deviations from the normal vote. Thus a different normal vote baseline was used when calculating the deviation for the two-party vote than in calculating the deviation for the three-party vote.

5. For two examples of scholarly works that cast doubt on the claims of religious right leaders concerning their influence on the 1980 presidential vote, see S. M. Lipset and Earl Raab, "The Election and the Evangelicals," *Commentary* 71 (March 1981): 25-31; and Arthur H. Miller and Martin P. Wattenberg, "Politics from the Pulpit: Religiosity and the 1980 Elections," *Economic Outlook USA* (Summer 1982): 61-64. The findings concerning the influence of the religious right on the 1980 congressional vote are more mixed.

6. For an explanation of these long- and short-term measures, see Richard W. Boyd, "Popular Control of Public Policy: A Normal Vote Analysis of the 1968 Election," *American Political Science Review* 66 (June 1972): 431-48. The long-term index (L) is the weighted average absolute deviation of the expected vote for each category of the independent variable (religion) from the expected vote for the total population. The more L deviates from zero, the greater will be the relationship between religion and the normal or expected vote. The short-term index (S) is formed by first calculating the deviation from the normal vote for each religious category. The S value is the weighted average absolute difference between this deviation for each religious category and that for the total population. The more S deviates from zero, the greater will be the relationship between religion and deviation from the expected vote. Only respondents who fell into one of our four religious categories were included in these calculations.

7. The existence of differences in the voting patterns of the religious groups in the South is all the more impressive when we consider the adjustment we have made in our denominational classification scheme for 1960 and 1968. This adjustment results in a number of moderate Protestants being lumped in with the conservatives in the South. Therefore, this conservative group probably stands out in its political behavior even more than our figures suggest.

8. In order to control for these three variables we have attempted to dichotomize them in a way that will maximize the number of cases in each category. In the case of income this meant using a different cutoff point for each year, since inflation and economic growth caused the average income to increase greatly over this 12-year period.

4

Religion and
the Presidential Candidates

INTRODUCTION

Our brief summary of American political history in Chapter 1 strongly suggested that one factor that has influenced the effect of religious beliefs on presidential voting has been the nature of the candidates nominated by the major political parties. The historical data seem to indicate that in a given presidential election year different combinations of candidates will not be equally likely to politicize the various religious cleavages inherent in American society. The survey data we have examined for the six most recent presidential elections have added further credence to this basic notion by showing that the nature and intensity of the religious effect can vary tremendously from one election to the next. For instance, the voting data indicate that an intense polarization occurred between liberal and conservative Protestants in 1972, but by 1976 this split had almost completely dwindled away. The short period of time between elections seems to suggest that the difference in the candidate pairings had a great deal to do with the difference in the religious effect. Nevertheless, this kind of evidence is not in itself adequate for reaching firm conclusions. What is needed is a more direct test of our hypothesis, which will hold the time factor constant.

Fortunately, for the last few presidential elections such a direct test is possible. In the most recent presidential election surveys carried out by the University of Michigan, a series of questions was asked in an attempt to measure overall public sentiment toward several of the major national political figures of these years. These questions asked respondents to assign each of these national figures a feeling-thermometer rating. The possible ratings ranged from a strongly positive 100 points to a strongly negative 0 points, with 50 points being a rating of neutral feeling. The utility of these ratings for our purposes stems from two basic facts. In the first place the relative thermometer ratings for the major party nominees serve as extremely accurate predictors of the actual vote.[1] In the second place, unlike with the actual vote, these thermometer ratings are available for many political figures who were not presidential nominees in a given year. This allows for the possibility that hypothetical or mock election outcomes can be constructed for various pairings of these major political figures.[2] In this way possible variations in the effect of religious beliefs on the vote due to differences in candidate pairings can be ascertained.

It is important, of course, that we try to limit ourselves to political figures who are well-known and have well-established political images.[3] Thermometer ratings for several such well-known individuals are available for each of the presidential election years from 1972 through 1980. Examination of mock election pairings for each of these three years should be sufficient to establish strong evidence to support or refute our proposition concerning the effect of the presidential candidates on the relationship between religious belief and presidential voting behavior.

ELECTION PAIRINGS AND THE RELIGIOUS EFFECT

For the 1972 election, thermometer ratings are available for a total of six well-known political figures. Aside from the actual major party nominees, Richard Nixon and George McGovern, they include Hubert Humphrey, Edmund Muskie, George Wallace, and Ted Kennedy. Humphrey, of course, had been the Democratic nominee in 1968, while Muskie had been the vice-presidential nominee in 1968 and the original front runner for the presidential nomination in 1972. Kennedy and Wallace had never been nominated for national office by one of the two major parties, but each had for very different reasons attained tremendous political visibility by 1972. Since Nixon was the only Republican in the bunch, a total of five election pairings can be formed (one real and four mock elections). The results are displayed in Table 4.1.

TABLE 4.1
Real versus Mock Elections, 1972, 1976, 1980
(in percentages)

Denominational Category	Candidate		
	1972		
	Real		
	McGovern	*Nixon*	*Dev.*
Liberal Protestants	26	74	−15
Moderate Protestants	24	76	−20
Conservative Protestants	20	80	−39
Catholics	38	62	−29
n of cases	1,258		
	Mock		
	Wallace	*Nixon*	*Dev.*
Liberal Protestants	20	80	−21
Moderate Protestants	24	76	−20
Conservative Protestants	41	59	−18
Catholics	26	74	−41
n of cases	1,203		
	Muskie	*Nixon*	*Dev.*
Liberal Protestants	22	78	−19
Moderate Protestants	20	80	−24
Conservative Protestants	14	86	−45
Catholics	38	62	−29
n of cases	1,121		
	Kennedy	*Nixon*	*Dev.*
Liberal Protestants	24	76	−17
Moderate Protestants	24	76	−20
Conservative Protestants	22	78	−37
Catholics	47	53	−20
n of cases	1,217		

Denominational Category	Candidate		
	Humphrey	*Nixon*	*Dev.*
Liberal Protestants	21	79	−20
Moderate Protestants	23	77	−21
Conservative Protestants	17	83	−42
Catholics	37	63	−30
n of cases	1,222		

1976

Real

	Carter	*Ford*	*Dev.*
Liberal Protestants	36	64	−5
Moderate Protestants	40	60	−5
Conservative Protestants	50	50	−7
Catholics	56	44	−9
n of cases	1,271		

Mock

	Carter	*Reagan*	*Dev.*
Liberal Protestants	45	55	+4
Moderate Protestants	46	54	+1
Conservative Protestants	52	48	−5
Catholics	61	39	−4
n of cases	1,221		

	Humphrey	*Reagan*	*Dev.*
Liberal Protestants	39	61	−2
Moderate Protestants	32	68	−13
Conservative Protestants	30	70	−27
Catholics	49	51	−16
n of cases	1,187		

Denominational Category	Candidate		
	Humphrey	*Ford*	*Dev.*
Liberal Protestants	25	75	−16
Moderate Protestants	26	74	−19
Conservative Protestants	26	74	−31
Catholics	44	56	−21
n of cases	1,198		
	Kennedy	*Reagan*	*Dev.*
Liberal Protestants	39	61	−2
Moderate Protestants	36	64	−5
Conservative Protestants	31	69	−26
Catholics	59	41	−6
n of cases	1,211		
	Kennedy	*Ford*	*Dev.*
Liberal Protestants	26	74	−15
Moderate Protestants	31	69	−14
Conservative Protestants	32	68	−25
Catholics	51	49	−14
n of cases	1,231		
	McGovern	*Reagan*	*Dev.*
Liberal Protestants	32	68	−9
Moderate Protestants	27	73	−18
Conservative Protestants	21	79	−36
Catholics	44	56	−21
n of cases	1,142		
	McGovern	*Ford*	*Dev.*
Liberal Protestants	23	77	−18
Moderate Protestants	22	78	−23
Conservative Protestants	19	81	−38
Catholics	37	63	−28
n of cases	1,154		

Denominational Category	Candidate		
	1980		
	Real		
	Carter	*Reagan*	*Dev.*
Liberal Protestants	34	66	−9
Moderate Protestants	29	71	−18
Conservative Protestants	42	58	−17
Catholics	43	57	−18
n of cases	634		
	Mock		
	Carter	*Ford*	*Dev.*
Liberal Protestants	35	65	−8
Moderate Protestants	37	63	−10
Conservative Protestants	51	49	−8
Catholics	49	51	−12
n of cases	604		
	Kennedy	*Reagan*	*Dev.*
Liberal Protestants	23	77	−20
Moderate Protestants	26	74	−21
Conservative Protestants	22	78	−37
Catholics	40	60	−21
n of cases	602		
	Kennedy	*Ford*	*Dev.*
Liberal Protestants	22	78	−21
Moderate Protestants	20	80	−27
Conservative Protestants	31	69	−28
Catholics	45	55	−16
n of cases	602		

Source: All of the tables in this chapter were compiled by the author.

Note: Each mock election for 1980 excludes Anderson votes.

One can easily determine that the effect of religion on the vote varies greatly across the five candidate pairings. In terms of deviation from the normal vote, the split between liberal and conservative Protestants varies only slightly when any of the four liberal candidates—McGovern, Humphrey, Muskie, or Kennedy—is matched against Richard Nixon (from 20 points for Kennedy to 26 points for Muskie). In each of these cases conservative Protestants are far more likely than liberal Protestants to deviate in the Republican direction. However, when Wallace is matched against Nixon the liberals are actually 3 points more likely to deviate in favor of the Republicans. Thus, this polarization between liberal and conservative Protestants varies by a total of 29 points across the election pairings. Catholic support for the Democratic candidate also varies widely, with Catholics deviating by 20 points in the Republican direction when Kennedy is nominated and 41 points in the same direction when Wallace is the nominee. As a result the polarization between Catholics and liberal Protestants ranges from a mere three points with Kennedy to a full 20 points with Wallace. Catholic support for McGovern, Muskie, and Humphrey is almost exactly equal, falling in between their support for Kennedy and Wallace. This is actually quite surprising, since Humphrey did far better among Catholics in 1968 than McGovern did in 1972. These findings seem to indicate a general growth of Catholic dissatisfaction with the mainstream of the Democratic party in the years between the elections of 1968 and 1972. More will be said about this apparent trend in the next section.

For the 1976 election, thermometer ratings are once again available for Hubert Humphrey, George McGovern, and Ted Kennedy, as well as for the actual Democratic nominee, Jimmy Carter. On the Republican side, ratings are available for the actual nominee, Gerald Ford, as well as for his leading opponent for the nomination, Ronald Reagan. This enables us to form a total of eight election pairings (one real and seven mock elections), which are displayed in Table 4.1. As with 1972, the importance of the candidate pairings in affecting the relationship between religion and the vote is readily apparent. In the actual election contest, between Jimmy Carter and Gerald Ford, virtually no religion effect was present. Each religious group deviated from the normal vote in approximately the same proportions. However, such is not the case with a number of the hypothetical pairings. In the race between Carter and Ford, conservative Protestants had been only 2 points more likely than the liberal Protestants to deviate from the normal vote in the Republican direction. When Ford is matched against Humphrey, Kennedy, and McGovern, the gap increases to 15, 10, and 20 points respectively. In addition, the substitution of Reagan for Ford on the Republican side further increases this polarization between the Protestant groups for pairings involving each of the Democratic candidates. Replacing Ford with Reagan increases this Protestant split from 2 to 9 points for the match with Carter, from 15 to 25 points for the match with Humphrey, from 10 to 24 points for the match with Kennedy, and from 20 to 27 points for the match with McGovern. It is obvious that a Reagan candidacy causes much more division in the Protestant camp than a Ford candidacy. Reagan seems to hold a particularly strong positive appeal for the conservative Protestants and a particularly strong negative appeal for their liberal counterparts.

The relative unpopularity of mainstream Democratic candidates among Catholics that began in 1972 continued into 1976. In the election pairings it is the newcomer, Jimmy Carter, who does best among this particular religious group. In the pairings involving Gerald Ford, Carter is able to pull down 56 percent of the vote. This compares with 51 percent for Kennedy, 44 percent for Humphrey, and a pitiful 37 percent for McGovern. Substituting Reagan for Ford increases Catholic support for each of the four Democratic candidates by 5 to 8 percentage points. This seems to indicate the relative unpopularity of Reagan, compared to Ford, among Catholics at this point in time. As a result of all this, the gaps between Catholics and each of the two polar Protestant groups vary widely across the eight election pairings.

What do the data tell us about the appeal of Catholic candidates among Catholic voters? In 1960 John Kennedy's Catholicism seemed to play a critical role in causing millions of Catholic voters to cast their ballots for the Democratic nominee. The findings of Table 4.1 suggest that this "Catholic" issue had died down considerably by the 1970s. In 1972 Ted Kennedy did better among Catholics than any of the other Democrats, but the other Catholic, Edmund Muskie, did not stand out this way. In both 1976 and 1980 Jimmy Carter did somewhat better among Catholics than Kennedy, although in 1976 Kennedy did better than the other candidates. Although these data clearly suggest a decline in the effect of Catholic group identification, they do not rule out the possibility that in a given election context a candidate's Catholicism could be an advantage in winning Catholic support.

For the 1980 election the available thermometer ratings allow us to pair Jimmy Carter and Ted Kennedy against Ronald Reagan and Gerald Ford (one real and three mock elections). Once again the magnitude of the religion effect varies widely across the election pairings. The actual contest between Carter and Reagan resulted in relatively small differences between the religious groups in terms of their deviation from the normal vote. This lack of religion effect does not change when Ford is substituted for Reagan in a match with Carter. However, things change considerably when Kennedy is substituted for Carter and matched with each of the Republican candidates. When this happens large polarizations develop between liberal and conservative Protestants on the one hand, and between Catholics and conservative Protestants on the other. This is especially true when Ted Kennedy is pitted against Ronald Reagan. The special appeal of Reagan among conservative Protestants, relative to the other religious groups, is once again demonstrated.

This, of course, leads us back to the question of whether the Reagan victory in 1980 was largely a result of a groundswell of support among conservative Protestants. The actual voting data reported in Chapter 3 cast grave doubt on the claims of the leadership of the religious right that their efforts on behalf of Reagan played a special role in the election outcome. The findings presented here can only add to this skepticism. The data from both 1976 and 1980 show that Reagan had indeed had a special relative appeal among conservative Protestants. But the effect of this appeal is heavily dependent on the nature of his Democratic opponent. Specifically, in both 1976 and 1980 the candidacy of Jimmy Carter was able to offset much of this relative Reagan popularity among this particular Protestant group. If Reagan had opposed different candidates—such as Humphrey in 1976 or Kennedy in 1980—he would have won overwhelmingly among conservative Protestants, causing countless numbers of them to desert the Democratic party. The key variable here seems to be the exact nature of the candidate pairing. This fact is of such importance that it makes any special organizational effort on the part of the new right religious groups seem trivial in comparison.

It can be seen then that modern survey data have allowed us to confirm the proposition that we derived from our examination of historical material. The impact of religious beliefs on presidential voting behavior is indeed highly dependent on the nature of the choice of candidates presented to the voters by the major political parties.

CHANGES IN CANDIDATE APPEAL OVER TIME

It has now been made clear that the major presidential candidates themselves play a major role in determining the nature and magnitude of the impact of religious beliefs on presidential voting. Thus far we have seen how much of a difference that variations in candidate pairings can make in any given election year. This, of course, has been the major goal of this chapter. Before moving on, however, it seems worthwhile to take a brief look at how the appeal of various candidates for each religious group has changed over time. Such an examination may offer us further clues as to the exact nature of the mechanisms by which religious beliefs have been affecting voting behavior in recent elections.

Such changes in the overall popularity of individual candidates among each religious group can be estimated by looking at changes in their thermometer ratings over time. The mean scores of these thermometer ratings for various major political figures are presented in Table 4.2. Among the numerous findings that can be derived from this table, one in particular stands out. In Chapter 3 we discussed the startling decline in Catholic support for the Democratic nominee between 1968 and 1972. Since this support increased dramatically in 1976, there was good reason to believe that this Catholic desertion was a temporary reaction to the candidacy of George McGovern. However, the data in Table 4.2 compel us to qualify this conclusion. By 1972 most of the mainstream Democratic candidates were doing badly among Catholics. Of particular interest is the decline in Catholic support for Hubert Humphrey over the four-year period. Support for Edmund Muskie among Catholics was every bit as weak as it was for Humphrey, while support for George McGovern was weaker still. Support for Ted Kennedy was slightly higher, but still far lower than the support for Humphrey in 1968. These facts seem to suggest that some sort of changes occurring in the Democratic party during this period were having an adverse effect on the party's traditional Catholic base of support. It should be said that any conclusions regarding change must be made with some caution since a meaningful thermometer

TABLE 4.2
Mean Thermometer Ratings by Religion, 1968, 1976, 1980 (in percentages)

Denominational Category		Year		
Hubert Humphrey				
	1968[a]	1968[b]	1972	1976
Liberal Protestants	58	59	50	49
Moderate Protestants	55	57	51	48
Conservative Protestants	49	59	43	45
Catholics	69	72	56	56
Richard Nixon				
		1968[a]	1968[b]	1972
Liberal Protestants		73	75	71
Moderate Protestants		73	75	75
Conservative Protestants		68	75	74
Catholics		64	65	66
George McGovern				
			1972	1976
Liberal Protestants			46	45
Moderate Protestants			41	42
Conservative Protestants			35	38
Catholics			50	49
George Wallace				
				1972
Liberal Protestants				49
Moderate Protestants				53
Conservative Protestants				66
Catholics				50
Edmund Muskie				
				1972
Liberal Protestants				49
Moderate Protestants				49
Conservative Protestants				42
Catholics				55

Denominational Category	Year			
Edward Kennedy				
	1972	1976	1980[a]	1980[b]
Liberal Protestants	44	46	37	37
Moderate Protestants	46	49	40	39
Conservative Protestants	41	45	39	38
Catholics	59	60	50	50
Jimmy Carter				
		1976	1980[a]	1980[b]
Liberal Protestants		55	48	48
Moderate Protestants		58	52	52
Conservative Protestants		63	56	57
Catholics		64	56	57
Gerald Ford				
		1976	1980[a]	1980[b]
Liberal Protestants		68	64	64
Moderate Protestants		66	65	65
Conservative Protestants		65	61	60
Catholics		60	59	59
Ronald Reagan				
		1976	1980[a]	1980[b]
Liberal Protestants		62	64	65
Moderate Protestants		62	61	62
Conservative Protestants		65	64	64
Catholics		58	57	59

[a]Three party.

[b]Two party (excludes Wallace and Anderson voters).

rating for 1968 is available only for Humphrey. In addition there was a significant decline in support for Humphrey among each of the other religious groups as well. However, the decline was clearly greatest among Catholics, thus acting to lessen the differences in candidate ratings between Catholics and the various Protestant groups.

It also seems to be the case that this negative trend among Catholics was not as temporary as we had previously thought. In 1976 Catholic support for Humphrey, McGovern, and Kennedy remained at the relatively low levels of 1972. In 1980 thermometer ratings of these particular candidates were available only in the case of Kennedy, but this Kennedy rating among Catholics showed a drastic decline between 1976 and 1980. All in all, mainstream Democratic political figures have had great difficulty appealing to Catholic voters in the years since 1968. The one exception seems to have been the newcomer, Jimmy Carter, whose Catholic support in 1976 was significantly higher than that of the other Democratic candidates. But even here Carter's 1976 rating was lower than Humphrey's had been in 1968. By 1980 it too had declined sharply, as had Carter's support among all of the religious groups.[4]

All of this suggests that a key turning point in the way that Catholics viewed the political world around them occurred between the years 1968 and 1972. The fact that the drop in Democratic support occurred more among this religious group than among the others leaves open the possibility that religious beliefs played an important role in this rather sudden turn of events. Thus, the falling off of Democratic support among Catholics after 1968 joins the growing polarization of liberal and conservative Protestants in the 1960s as important political trends that seem to have been somehow related to religious beliefs. In Chapter 5 we will attempt to determine the exact nature of this relationship.

NOTES

1. The strong predictive power provided by these thermometer ratings in regard to the actual voting outcomes can be tested by creating mock elections that pair the actual presidential nominees and comparing these to the actual voting results. Such a procedure shows that the thermometers are extremely accurate predictors of the actual vote for the elections of 1968, 1972, and 1976. For 1980 the predicted outcome provided by the thermometers is much less on target, probably because of the inordinate amount of last-minute

switching that went on in the days before the election but after the survey was conducted. The view that the surprisingly large margin of Ronald Reagan's victory was a result of last-minute movement away from Carter is supported by the fact that the thermometer ratings systematically overestimate the Carter vote.

2. A relatively simple method was used to create the mock election results. For each candidate pairing, a respondent was credited as voting for the candidate to whom he gave the higher thermometer rating. For those respondents who rated the candidates equally, the vote was divided evenly between the two candidates. As mentioned, this procedure provides extremely accurate predictions of the actual vote for each election except 1980.

3. For each year we tried to stick only to political figures who were very well known. The popular images of politicians who are not well known are likely to change significantly during the course of a long and highly visible presidential campaign. This is likely to be less true of those whose images are already well established. Therefore, an extra note of realism is provided by dealing only with those who fall in the latter category. This is not to say that the relative popularity of these well-known politicians would not have undergone any change had they been nominated and subjected to a general election campaign. The mock election estimates that involve such political figures are not to be taken as exact estimates of how the election would have turned out had they been nominated. For our purposes all that matters is that the mock elections be realistic enough to allow us to test the impact of changing combinations of presidential candidates on the relationship between religious beliefs and the presidential vote.

4. Carter's advantage over Hubert Humphrey and George McGovern in 1976 occurred mainly among conservative Protestants and Catholics. This seems to indicate that he somehow managed to avoid the special antagonisms that had haunted the other major Democratic figures in regard to the conservative Protestants since the mid-1960s and in regard to the Catholics since 1972. The result was that religion had little impact on the 1976 election. This fact, of course, was established in Chapter 3. Between 1976 and 1980 Carter's support declined rather evenly among all the religious groups. Thus, religion had little impact on the 1980 election as well. It is interesting to note here that the thermometers suggest that the Reagan victory was not so much the result of any growth in the popularity of Ronald Reagan from 1976 to 1980 as it was from the fairly sharp decline in the popularity of Carter among all of the religious groups. This is yet one more piece of evidence to counter the conservative claims of an electoral mandate in the 1980 presidential election.

5

Religion and Political Attitudes

INTRODUCTION

It is sometimes said that the most baffling phenomenon in all the universe is the human mind. In fact it is probably fair to say that man now knows more about the secrets of the most distant of stars than he does about the mysteries of his own mental world. The human psyche is a perplexing web consisting of numerous elements that fit together in an overall structure of enormous complexity. Much of modern psychology is concerned with mapping the pattern of elements that make up this structure. Included among these elements are such things as beliefs and attitudes.

In their attempt to understand the relationships between these various aspects of the human psyche, social psychologists have introduced the concept of centrality. According to these theorists not all of the attitudes and beliefs held by a given individual are of equal centrality or importance to him. While some will play a key role in influencing his perceptions of the world around him, others will remain largely on his mental periphery. These more peripheral attitudes and beliefs will tend to play a less important role in influencing the individual's actual behavior. In addition they are far more likely to change in response to new information than those in the center. On occasion an individual will hold attitudes and beliefs that are inconsistent with one another. If these attitudes and beliefs reach a certain threshold of salience, the inconsistency between them will result in the creation of psychic tension. When this occurs the individual is likely to change his more peripheral beliefs in order to make them more consistent with those that are more central to him. Thus, in terms of an overall psychological structure, influence or causality will generally flow from the center outward.

This type of social psychological theory has tremendous relevance for our analysis. Thus far we have been able to provide strong evidence that religious beliefs influence the presidential voting behavior of a good many Americans. Our concern in this chapter is with explaining exactly how this link comes about. In Chapter 2 we showed how various religious groups in America differ along a number of belief dimensions. But how do these beliefs come to influence the presidential vote? It seems clear that we are as yet missing a step. In order to influence voting behavior religious beliefs must first influence the political attitudes that have been shown to affect the vote directly.[1] Social psychological theory provides us with a general explanation of how this can occur. All available evidence suggests that for the vast majority of Americans religious beliefs are far more central than the beliefs they hold about politics. Thus, when political attitudes can somehow be related to religious beliefs, the latter will influence the former. It is our task to explain the specifics of how this relationship between religious beliefs and political attitudes comes about.

Since they may play a central role in the psychological structures of most Americans, we can expect religious beliefs to change only slowly. This means that at the societal level the distribution of religious beliefs in the population will also be slow to change. Therefore it can be expected that the fairly rapid shifts that seem to occur in the relationship between religious beliefs and voting behavior are not generally the result of religious change. Rather it would seem that such rapid shifts are the result of changes in the political attitudes that intervene between religious beliefs and the voting decision. Past research has suggested that such political attitudes are highly responsive to changes in the political environments of individuals in the electorate, particularly to changes at the elite level of politics.[2] These attitudes pertain to the candidates and issues to which the voter is exposed at a given point in time.

However, it would be incorrect to conceive of the individual voting decision as being totally reactive in nature. Though voters are highly dependent on the political stimuli to which they are exposed, different voters exposed to essentially the same stimuli are likely to react in quite different ways. This is because different individuals bring with them very different psychological structures through which these political stimuli must be processed. An important part of these structures is the set of beliefs that make up an individual's overall religious perspective. Therefore political attitudes are likely to be influenced by religious beliefs; but this process of religious influence will vary greatly over time. At times the dominant political stimuli will have little relevance to the religious beliefs of the vast majority of voters. The result will be that the emerging distribution of political attitudes in the electorate will be largely unrelated to religious beliefs. At such times we can expect religion to have little influence on the vote. At other times the nature of the dominant political stimuli to which voters are exposed will be such that many of them will be able to bring their religious beliefs into play. The result in this case will be a distribution of political attitudes that is highly related to the distribution of religious beliefs in the population. The ultimate effect will be that religion will be a major factor in influencing the partisan decisions of many voters.[3]

Thus we are postulating a kind of causal chain in which religious beliefs influence political attitudes, which in turn influence the vote. Much has been written about the relationship between political attitudes and the vote. Our concern in this chapter is to examine the part of the chain that remains largely unstudied: the relationship between religious beliefs and political attitudes. For reasons of practicality we have decided to focus on one presidential election, that of 1972. This particular year was chosen because it was one of the years in which the effect of religion on the presidential vote seemed to be quite strong. However, where it seems warranted we will occasionally examine attitude questions from other election years. In addition, later on in the chapter we will examine in a more systematic fashion the elections of 1968 and 1976. This approach will enable us to accomplish a number of goals. First, it will allow us to examine very closely the relationship between religious beliefs and political attitudes at a single point in time. Second, it will enable us to test the hypotheses laid out in Chapter 2 concerning the ways that different kinds of religious beliefs affect specific types of political attitudes. Finally, it will provide us an opportunity to attempt to explain the major religious-political trends uncovered in chapters 3 and 4: the increasing polarization between liberal and conservative Protestants in the 1960s, the sudden movement of Catholics away from the Democratic party in 1972, and the sudden decline of the religion effect in 1976.

RELIGION AND SOCIAL AND ECONOMIC ISSUES

In Chapter 2 it was shown how the four major religious groups in our study differ along three separate dimensions of religious belief. From these combinations of belief differences we were able to develop a series of hypotheses concerning the development of certain kinds of political attitudes among the members of each group. These hypotheses can now be tested using data from the 1972 presidential election study of the University of Michigan.

The first set of hypotheses dealt with attitudes regarding what we have referred to as the social or economic type of issue. By social and economic issues we mean all issues that in some fashion center around the idea of using government to aid those who seem to be somehow disadvantaged by the way American society is currently structured. This disadvantage can take many forms. It may apply to the job market, the educational system, or any other walk of life. The specific ways to use government to offset these disadvantages can vary greatly and each can become a political issue in its own right. What they all have in common is the notion of social or political altruism. In order to have a realistic possibility of succeeding, these proposed government efforts will usually require the support of a large number of people who do not directly benefit from them. This is where religious beliefs can come into play. As has been previously shown, there are vast differences among the major religious groups regarding the emphasis they place on this sort of altruism or ethicalism. Specifically, all other things being equal we can expect Catholics and liberal Protestants to be considerably more supportive of these types of programs than their conservative Protestant counterparts. However, it is necessary to mention here an important type of political issue that does not fall into this category. These are the issues that are based on economic self-interest rather than altruism. On an issue such as the relative distribution of the tax burden, for instance, we can expect class to emerge as a powerful counterweight to religion. This is important because at least among Protestants class and religious belief can potentially work against one another. Of course, issues may not fall neatly into one category or another. It is possible for an issue to elicit both economic self-interest and religious altruism. Therefore we will attempt to distinguish between those issues that can be expected to elicit responses based mainly on religiously derived altruism, those that can be expected to be based mainly on economic or class self-interest, and those that fall somewhere in between.

An example of an issue we would expect to elicit responses that are influenced by religious beliefs is civil rights. Yet here we must be careful to consider exactly how this issue has been defined at a given point in time. By 1972 numerous specific issues that were in various ways related to racial concerns had made their way onto the political agenda. Some of these we would have expected to elicit responses that were based largely on religiously inspired altruism, while others probably appealed more to class self-interest. During the early years of the civil rights movement the specific issues generally involved the very basic question of whether integration was in itself a desirable goal. The issue came to be presented by civil rights leaders in terms of basic social justice. Because of this we could expect religious beliefs to play a major role in the formation of public opinion. For most Catholics and liberal Protestants religious beliefs provided a definite cue as to the proper attitude response. Such blatant discrimination was quite obviously inconsistent with their interpretation of Christian duty as requiring each person to be concerned with achieving at least some minimal form of social justice for all. For most conservative Protestants, on the other hand, no such ethical command existed. For this reason we could expect members of this group to have been far less likely than the others to endorse social changes designed to bring about basic racial integration.

Fortunately these expectations can easily be tested with the 1972 data. Included in this year was a question that simply asked respondents whether they favored desegregation, strict segregation, or something in between. The mean responses to this question are broken down by religious category in Table 5.1. As with all of the other issue tables that follow, the results of applying a regional control are also displayed. This procedure is rendered necessary because of the disproportionate concentration of conservative Protestants in the South. In some cases additional controls for a class variable—income—will also be instituted. The exact reason for this will become clearer as our analysis unfolds.

TABLE 5.1

Integration

Does R favor desegregation, strict segregation, or something in between?
Responses: 1. Desegregation 3. In Between 5. Segregation

Denominational Category	Region				
	North		South		Overall
Liberal Protestants	2.25	(+.09)[a]	2.45	(−.34)	2.29
Moderate Protestants	2.26	(+.08)	2.61	(−.20)	2.31
Conservative Protestants	2.51	(−.37)	3.50	(−.01)	3.01 L, C[b]
Catholics	2.25	(+.10)	2.47	(−.31)	2.28
Overall	2.28		2.91		2.41
n of cases	1,227				

Controlled for Income
Less Than $10,000

Liberal Protestants	2.26	(+.06)	2.83	(0.00)	2.37
Moderate Protestants	2.54	(+.18)	2.52	(−.47)	2.53
Conservative Protestants	2.51	(−.46)	3.65	(+.05)	3.14
Catholics	2.43	(+.16)	2.48	(−.42)	2.44
Overall	2.43		3.06		2.60
n of cases	544				

$10,000 and over

Liberal Protestants	2.27	(+.10)	2.20	(−.54)	2.26
Moderate Protestants	1.98	(−.02)	2.77	(+.20)	2.09
Conservative Protestants	2.50	(−.23)	3.27	(−.03)	2.82
Catholics	2.18	(+.06)	2.44	(−.25)	2.21
Overall	2.18		2.75		2.27
n of cases	650				

[a]The figures in parentheses are the deviations from the expected cell values.

[b]The letters L and C after the conservative Protestants indicate statistically significant differences between this group and the liberal Protestants and Catholics, respectively, at the .05 level.

Source: All of the tables in this chapter were compiled by the author.

The results of Table 5.1 generally bear out our predictions about the relationship between religious belief and general attitudes toward racial desegregation. Liberal Protestants and Catholics were far more likely than conservative Protestants to favor desegregation. The differences in mean ratings between religious groups are quite impressive.[4] The data seem to indicate that both religion and region exercised significant independent effects on the development of mass attitudes toward the general desegregation issue. However, these data also hint at some sort of interactive effect between these two variables. In order to test for this the row and column means from the table were used to estimate expected values for each cell. Any deviations from these expected values would signify an inter-active effect. These deviations are displayed in parentheses following each of the actual cell values. They do in fact seem to indicate an interactive effect. Differences among religious groups were much greater in the South than in the North. The combination of living in the South and being a conservative Protestant greatly increased the chances of a person being a segregationist.

Defined this way, civil rights represents an almost "pure type" of social or economic issue. That is to say, there was little reason to have expected class interests to act as a counterweight to religion in affecting the issue results. Those people of high economic status had little to lose by being supportive of general desegregation. In fact further controls show that there was some tendency for support of desegregation to increase with income, although these controls do not explain away the apparent religion effect. However, many social and economic issues will not be quite so pure. It is possible for an issue to elicit responses that are based both on religiously inspired altruism and class self-interest. Of course, there may be certain issues on which the effects of class self-interest will be domi-nant. The differences among these various types of social and eco-nomic issues can probably be illustrated best with real-life examples.

We have already seen that the general desegregation issue seems to fit closely our description of a pure religious issue. What then would be an example of a pure class-based issue? While a completely pure class-based issue may not exist, the conflict over government job guarantees may fall largely within this theoretical category. It is probably fair to say that since the onslaught of the Great Depression and the New Deal the general jobs question has aroused a significant amount of class-based conflict. Thus a general desegregation question that makes no mention of jobs could be expected to elicit responses based largely on religious beliefs, while a general jobs question that makes no mention of race could be expected to elicit responses based largely on class. It follows then that an issue question that involved both racial and job-market concerns could be expected to elicit both types of responses.

Examples of each of these three types of issue questions can be found in the 1972 election study. As stated earlier, mean responses to a general desegregation question are displayed in Table 5.1. Table 5.2 displays the mean responses to a question concerning the role of government in guaranteeing job security for all. Finally, Table 5.3 displays the mean responses to our mixed-issue example, one that concerns the role of government in guaranteeing fair treatment for blacks in the job market.

In order to provide us with confidence that these three real-life issues are actually representative of our three theoretical categories, two measures have been taken. In the first place, controls for class (income) have been instituted for each issue and have been displayed in the relevant issue table. In addition the overall effects of class on mean responses to each of the three questions have been summarized in Table 5.4. It can be seen immediately that the net effect of class varied widely across the three issues. On the general integration issue religion seems to have exerted a considerably more powerful effect than social class, with the differences among religious groups within each income bracket being larger than the differences across income categories. In this case the relatively small effect of class actually worked in the same direction as religion since the more liberal religious groups were also those with the highest average incomes. Such was not the case with the "pure" jobs question as religion and class worked to offset one another. In this case opposition to government intervention in the job market increased with income among three of the four religious groups. The lone exception was the liberal Protestant group, whose members actually became more liberal as their incomes rose. Within each income category a significant religion effect seems to have been present, with Catholics and liberal Protestants being considerably more liberal than the conservative Protestants. The only exception to this usual pattern of religious influence was the lower-income liberal Protestant group, whose members were surprisingly conservative. Partly because of this anomaly the overall religion effect was not strong enough to overcome the relatively more powerful class factor. Thus, this

TABLE 5.2
Guarantee Jobs

Should the federal government guarantee jobs?
Responses: From 1. Government see to job and good standard of living.
    through 7. Government let each person get ahead on his own.

Denominational Category	Region				
	North		South		Overall
Liberal Protestants	4.60	(+.05)	4.65	(−.18)	4.61
Moderate Protestants	4.53	(−.04)	5.19	(+.34)	4.63
Conservative Protestants	4.70	(0.00)	4.81	(−.17)	4.76 C
Catholics	4.21	(+.08)	4.13	(−.28)	4.19
Overall	4.45		4.73		4.51
n of cases	580				
	Controlled for Income				
	Less than $10,000				
Liberal Protestants	4.74	(+.02)	4.90	(−.06)	4.78
Moderate Protestants	4.40	(−.02)	4.83	(+.17)	4.48
Conservative Protestants	3.91	(−.23)	4.50	(+.12)	4.20
Catholics	3.88	(+.06)	3.86	(−.20)	3.88
Overall	4.24		4.48		4.30
n of cases	232				
	$10,000 and Over				
Liberal Protestants	4.54	(+.11)	4.42	(−.48)	4.52
Moderate Protestants	4.63	(−.05)	5.57	(+.42)	4.77
Conservative Protestants	5.27	(+.12)	5.21	(−.41)	5.24
Catholics	4.37	(+.08)	4.50	(−.26)	4.38
Overall	4.56		5.03		4.65
n of cases	333				

TABLE 5.3
Job Integration

Should the government in Washington see to it that black people get fair treatment in jobs or leave these matters to the states and local communities?
Responses: 1. See to it that black people get fair treatment.
   5. Leave to states and local communities.

	Region				
	North		South		Overall
Denominational Category					
Liberal Protestants	3.22	(+.04)	3.49	(−.13)	3.28
Moderate Protestants	2.99	(0.00)	3.67	(+.24)	3.09
Conservative Protestants	3.46	(−.05)	3.76	(−.19)	3.61 L, C
Catholics	2.92	(+.11)	2.79	(−.46)	2.91
Overall	3.07		3.51		3.17
n of cases	972				

Controlled for Income
Less than $10,000

Liberal Protestants	3.14	(−.01)	3.67	(+.12)	3.26
Moderate Protestants	3.07	(+.01)	3.61	(+.15)	3.17
Conservative Protestants	3.48	(+.07)	3.55	(−.26)	3.52
Catholics	2.84	(+.08)	3.00	(−.16)	2.87
Overall	3.08		3.48		3.19
n of cases	433				

$10,000 and Over

Liberal Protestants	3.34	(+.04)	3.67	(−.20)	3.40
Moderate Protestants	2.90	(0.00)	3.67	(+.20)	3.00
Conservative Protestants	3.40	(+.24)	4.15	(−.06)	3.74
Catholics	2.96	(+.14)	2.50	(−.89)	2.92
Overall	3.07		3.64		3.17
n of cases	513				

TABLE 5.4
Three Issues by Income

Income Category	Issue		
	Integration	Job Integration	Guarantee Jobs
Less than $10,000	2.60	3.19	4.30
$10,000 and over	2.27	3.17	4.65

Cell entries are the mean response for each of the three issue questions in each income category. They are taken directly from Tables 5.1 through 5.3.

general jobs issue does somewhat approximate a pure class-related type of social or economic issue.

On purely theoretical grounds we could expect the third question to fall in between the other two. This job integration question, which asks about the propriety of government efforts to help blacks in the job market, would seem to include both racial and job-market components. As such we could expect both class and religion to exert significant effects on responses to it. The data from Table 5.4 are consistent with this expectation, since the effect of class on this issue seems to have been offset by some other factor. Further information is supplied by Table 5.3, which indicates the presence of a significant religion effect that easily overwhelms the very slight class effect that existed among all groups but the moderate Protestants. Still some kind of larger class effect may be indicated by the surprising conservatism of the liberal Protestants relative to the Catholics. This difference did not occur for the general integration question and therefore suggests that more than a racial component was being tapped.[5] All in all, the evidence does seem to at least suggest that the job integration issue did in fact tap more than one issue component and therefore stands as an example of the highly impure or mixed-issue type.

In general, it can be said that the less a social or economic type of issue involves some kind of appeal to economic class interest, the stronger the net effect of religious beliefs will be on the formation of attitudes regarding that issue.[6] The relative strength of social class and religion on the formation of issue attitudes will be highly dependent on exactly how an issue is defined at any given point in time.

Finally, some religion effect seems to have been present in determining responses to four other issues of the social or economic type: minority aid, the general issue of school integration, urban

TABLE 5.5
Minority Aid
Minority group aid scale.
Responses: From 1. Government should help minority groups.
    through 7. Minority groups should help themselves.

	Region				
Denominational Category	*North*		*South*		*Overall*
Liberal Protestants	4.22	(+.07)	4.50	(−.27)	4.28
Moderate Protestants	4.48	(+.05)	4.96	(−.09)	4.56
Conservative Protestants	4.51	(−.28)	5.33	(−.08)	4.92 L, C
Catholics	4.20	(+.09)	4.51	(−.22)	4.24
Overall	4.32		4.94		4.45
n of cases	1,130				

unrest, and the specific issue of busing to achieve school desegregation (see Tables 5.5 through 5.8). This religion effect could have been expected since all of these issues incorporate an important racial or civil rights component. Whatever class effects may have been present for each of the four issue questions were obviously

TABLE 5.6
School Integration
Does R think that the government in Washington should see to it that white and black children go to the same schools or stay out of this area as it is not its business?
Responses: 1. See to it. . . . 5. Stay out of this area. . . .

	Region				
Denominational Category	*North*		*South*		*Overall*
Liberal Protestants	3.34	(+.06)	3.67	(−.19)	3.40
Moderate Protestants	3.26	(+.06)	3.62	(−.16)	3.32
Conservative Protestants	3.65	(−.17)	4.22	(−.18)	3.94 L, C
Catholics	3.28	(+.06)	3.84	(+.04)	3.34
Overall	3.33		3.91		3.45
n of cases	1,040				

TABLE 5.7
Urban Unrest

Urban unrest scale.
Responses: From 1. Solve problems of poverty and unemployment.
through 7. Use all available force.

	Region		
Denominational Category	*North*	*South*	*Overall*
Liberal Protestants	3.10 (−.04)	3.88 (+.12)	3.27
Moderate Protestants	3.38 (−.04)	4.40 (+.36)	3.55
Conservative Protestants	3.60 (+.08)	3.72 (−.42)	3.65 C
Catholics	3.07 (+.11)	3.29 (−.29)	3.09
Overall	3.23	3.85	3.36
n of cases	536		

not large enough to offset the significant effect of religious beliefs. The more ethically based religious groups (the Catholics and the liberal Protestants) were considerably more likely than the conservative Protestants to favor government aid for minority groups and federal government intervention to bring about school integration.

TABLE 5.8
Busing

School busing scale.
Responses: From 1. Bus to achieve integration.
through 7. Keep children in neighborhood schools.

	Region		
Denominational Category	*North*	*South*	*Overall*
Liberal Protestants	6.22 (−.05)	6.80 (+.25)	6.33
Moderate Protestants	6.48 (+.03)	6.66 (−.07)	6.51
Conservative Protestants	6.64 (+.03)	6.69 (−.20)	6.67 L, C
Catholics	6.40 (+.03)	6.63 (−.02)	6.43
Overall	6.41	6.69	6.47
n of cases	1,185		

On the question of how to deal with urban unrest, Catholics and liberal Protestants were considerably more likely than conservative Protestants to favor the liberal approach, which emphasizes solving problems of poverty and unemployment over the use of force. However, responses to the busing question were unlike any we have seen thus far. On this issue the small religion effect that seems to have been present is rendered meaningless by the overwhelming opposition of all the religious groups to busing policy. In terms of actual voting behavior the busing issue is one that could have had the effect of making the various religious groups more alike. In this regard it runs counter to the other issues we have examined, which on the whole display the potential for causing very different voting patterns among the major religious groups. We shall keep this in mind when we attempt to relate our issue findings to various electoral trends later in this chapter.

RELIGION AND MORAL ISSUES

The second set of hypotheses developed in Chapter 2 concerned the relationship between religious beliefs and attitudes toward what we have referred to as the moral type of issue. It was suggested that while attitudes regarding social and economic issues will be greatly influenced by the ethical dimension of religious belief, attitudes regarding moral issues will be strongly related to both religious orthodoxy and evangelism. Specifically, it was hypothesized that the tendency of conservative Protestants to both adhere to a rigid form of morality and feel compelled to spread this morality to others will incline them to favor government intervention to enforce their version of social morality. On the other hand, the low scores of the liberal Protestants on both of these belief dimensions should predispose them to oppose using the government for this purpose. The fairly high level of orthodoxy found among Catholics should be offset largely by their overwhelming rejection of evangelism, thus making them about as likely as the liberal Protestants to oppose government intervention in the moral realm.

These hypotheses regarding the moral issues cannot be as thoroughly tested as those regarding the social and economic issues because of the limited number of relevant issue questions included in the 1972 election study. Nevertheless, one question included in the survey—pertaining to the legalization of abortion—does seem to fall into this particular issue category. In addition, two other issue questions from the 1980 survey—pertaining to prayer in public schools and the Equal Rights Amendment—also seem to be suitable for our purposes.[7] Of these three, probably the most clear-cut example of a moral type of issue is the one regarding the role of prayer in public schools. Since the U.S. Supreme Court ruled in 1962 that organized prayer in public schools is an unconstitutional violation of the separation of church and state, there have been a number of political attempts to circumvent the Court's decision through such means as the passage of a new amendment to the Constitution. Those backing school prayer have tended to argue that America was meant to be essentially a religious country and that the removal of prayer from public schools has helped to loosen the moral fabric of American society. Their opponents, on the other hand, have argued that allowing organized prayer in state-supported educational institutions inevitably amounts to government endorsement of a particular religious tradition.

Public opinion polls have consistently shown that a large majority of Americans favor some form of prayer in public schools. Nevertheless, we could expect some variation in this support among members of the major religious groups. Specifically, the high degree of both orthodoxy and evangelism found among conservative Protestants should make members of this group more prone than either Catholics or liberal Protestants to take a position in favor of school prayer. The data in Table 5.9 seem to confirm these expectations, with significant differences between groups occurring in the expected direction. Though religious group differences were present in both regions of the country, these were generally greater in the South, indicating once again the possibility of an interactive effect between religion and region.

A somewhat less pure example of a moral type of issue concerns the proposed passage of the Equal Rights Amendment. For some this controversy might seem to have little if anything to do with morality. Yet a closer inspection of the conflicts surrounding the proposed amendment reveals a highly important moral dimension. For its proponents the Equal Rights Amendment (ERA) represents a chance to render unconstitutional in one clean sweep dozens of national and state laws that discriminate between individuals on the basis of sex. To many of these proponents these laws represent the legal underpinnings of a traditional cultural system that limits the freedom of individuals by assigning them to narrow and predetermined social roles. It is probably fair to say that in the American context this traditional cultural system is at least in part an outgrowth of traditional or orthodox Christianity. This latter fact has not been lost on the new right religious leaders who have attempted to make the amendment's defeat an important element in their great moral crusade. Thus, although passage of the ERA requires a great deal of political action, it can be seen in part as an indirect attempt to provide for the further separation of church and state. As such we could expect the highly evangelistic and orthodox conservative Protestants to be considerably more likely than the liberal Protestants to oppose the amendment. For Catholics we could expect relatively high orthodoxy with its possible conservatizing influence on attitudes about sex roles to be largely offset by an extreme rejection of evangelism. Therefore, Catholics should rank near to the liberal Protestants in their support of the amendment. The data in Table 5.10 offer evidence to support each of these hypotheses. Though Southerners were considerably more conservative than Northerners, in both sections of the country large differences appeared among the religious groups regarding their attitudes toward this issue.

TABLE 5.9
School Prayer

Should there be prayer in public schools?

Responses: 1. Schools should be allowed to start each day with a prayer.
           3. Qualified response. (Prayer acceptable only if silent prayer/not mandatory for students/general universal statement not tied to any one sect/and so on.)
           5. Religion does not belong in the schools.

	Region				
Denominational Category	*North*		*South*		*Overall*
Liberal Protestants	2.09	(−.04)	1.52	(−.03)	1.97
Moderate Protestants	2.27	(+.03)	1.60	(−.05)	2.08
Conservative Protestants	1.70	(+.12)	1.14	(+.14)	1.42 L, C
Catholics	1.92	(−.14)	1.79	(+.31)	1.90
Overall	2.03		1.45		1.87
n of cases	583				

TABLE 5.10
Equal Rights Amendment

Do you approve or disapprove of the proposed Equal Rights Amendment to the Constitution, sometimes called the ERA Amendment?
Responses: 1. Strongly approve.
               2. Not strongly approve.
               4. Not strongly disapprove.
               5. Strongly disapprove.

	Region		
Denominational Category	*North*	*South*	*Overall*
Liberal Protestants	2.59 (−.01)	3.10 (+.10)	2.70
Moderate Protestants	3.05 (+.02)	3.40 (−.13)	3.13
Conservative Protestants	3.31 (+.01)	3.50 (−.20)	3.40 L, C
Catholics	2.76 (+.07)	2.91 (−.18)	2.79
Overall	2.88	3.28	2.98
n of cases	612		

     The final moral question deals with the controversial topic of abortion. In Chapter 2 we predicted that the breakdown of religious groups on this issue would not quite fit the usual pattern for moral issues. The divergence from this pattern should come among the Catholics who normally are paired with the liberal Protestants in opposition to government intervention in the moral realm. It will be recalled that this usual pairing results from the rejection of evangelism by both of these groups. But it must be kept in mind that Catholics and liberal Protestants arrive at their common policy positions in very different ways. In terms of personal morality, the average Catholic is considerably more traditional or orthodox than the average liberal Protestant. Thus, the alliance is made possible only by the tendency of Catholics to distinguish between personal and public morality. It is the lack of such a tendency among conservative Protestants that usually puts them in opposition to these other two groups on moral issues.

     Yet the case can be made that as moral issues go the abortion issue is rather unique. The orthodox Christian position on abortion, reinforced among Catholics by extraordinary efforts on the part of the Catholic clergy, is that the act of abortion is equivalent to the murder of an innocent human being. Therefore, for Catholics abortion becomes a moral question of the gravest concern. It is the exceptional gravity of the matter that makes the abortion issue different from other moral issues. Laws against abortion are seen by those who believe in the church's position not as a violation of the separation of church and state, but rather as the only effective means of protecting the lives of the unborn (ethicalism). For this reason we could expect that many Catholics will join the conservative Protestants in opposition to legalized abortion. On the other hand the low level of orthodoxy among liberal Protestants should enable them to take their usual stand in opposition to government intervention in the moral realm. Thus the survey data should show that both Catholics and conservative Protestants tended to be more conservative on this issue than the liberal Protestants. Once again the data seem to confirm our hypotheses[8] (see Table 5.11). Abortion thus ranks as the only issue among those we have examined on which Catholics were significantly more conservative than another religious group. This is something to keep in mind when we attempt to explain the sudden massive desertion of Catholics from the Democratic party in the 1972 presidential race.

TABLE 5.11
Abortion

When should abortion be allowed?
Responses: From 1. Abortion should never be permitted.
      through 4. Abortion should never be forbidden.

	Region		
Denominational Category	*North*	*South*	*Overall*
Liberal Protestants	2.84 (−.02)	2.67 (+.06)	2.81
Moderate Protestants	2.76 (−.02)	2.56 (+.03)	2.73
Conservative Protestants	2.41 (+.06)	2.19 (+.09)	2.30 L
Catholics	2.36 (−.02)	2.07 (−.06)	2.33
Overall	2.60	2.35	2.55
n of cases	1,226		

RELIGION AND FOREIGN POLICY ISSUES

Thus far we have avoided making any predictions about how religious beliefs may be related to attitudes regarding foreign policy issues. This is because the logical link between the religious belief dimensions that we have examined and foreign policy attitudes does not seem to be as obvious as the link between these same belief dimensions and attitudes toward moral or social and economic types of issues. Nevertheless, such a link between religious beliefs and attitudes toward this other issue area is not impossible to conceive. Some foreign policy issues involve a choice between placing emphasis on the use of force to achieve national ends and emphasizing more peaceful means of achieving the same purposes. Such a choice may be influenced by one's religious beliefs regarding the proper behavior between human beings. Specifically, it may very well be that the more emphasis an individual places on man-to-man ethicalism in guiding his behavior the less willing he will be to support foreign policy decisions that are based on the use of force. In addition to this ethicalism dimension, the other belief dimensions may also be of relevance. We have previously suggested that the strong emphasis placed on both orthodoxy and evangelism by the conservative Protestants results in a view of the world that draws a clear distinction between good and evil, the righteous and the wicked. Such a general religious orientation, if translated into a foreign policy perspective that draws sharp distinctions between righteous and wicked nations, could result in a very uncompromising and hawkish view of America's proper role in the international arena. Both of these potential religious influences on foreign policy attitudes should work in the same direction. When specific foreign policy issues are defined in ways that make these religious influences relevant to attitude formation, we can expect liberal Protestants and Catholics to take considerably more dovish stands than those who adhere to conservative Protestant principles.

These hypotheses can be tested with two different foreign policy questions from the 1972 presidential election study. These questions deal with the proper policy of the United States in Vietnam and the proper level of military spending (see Tables 5.12 and 5.13). Each of them involves a choice between a dovish and a hawkish policy stand. In both cases the predicted results occur, with Catholics and liberal Protestants being considerably more inclined to favor the dovish position than the conservative Protestants. As with all of the other specific issues we have examined, large differences among the religious groups remain even when controls are applied for region.

TABLE 5.12
Vietnam

Vietnam withdrawal scale.
Responses: From 1. Immediate withdrawal.
    through 7. Complete military victory.

Denominational Category	Region				Overall
	North		South		
Liberal Protestants	3.81	(+.08)	3.54	(−.34)	3.76
Moderate Protestants	3.68	(−.05)	4.17	(+.29)	3.76
Conservative Protestants	4.62	(+.26)	4.10	(−.41)	4.39 L, C
Catholics	3.80	(−.01)	4.21	(+.25)	3.84
Overall	3.86		4.01		3.89
n of cases	581				

Thus the survey data offer clear evidence that religious beliefs can have a strong influence on the development of a number of different types of political attitudes. With this in mind we can now set about to attempt to explain some of our major findings regarding the voting patterns of the major religious groups in recent presidential elections.

TABLE 5.13
Military Spending

Should military spending be cut?
Responses: 1. Cut military spending.
    5. Continue spending at least at present level.

Denominational Category	Region				Overall
	North		South		
Liberal Protestants	3.25	(+.09)	3.67	(−.21)	3.31
Moderate Protestants	3.48	(0.00)	4.41	(+.21)	3.63
Conservative Protestants	3.86	(−.02)	4.19	(−.41)	4.03 L, C
Catholics	3.25	(+.07)	3.96	(+.06)	3.33
Overall	3.38		4.10		3.53
n of cases	606				

RELIGIOUS BELIEFS, POLITICAL ATTITUDES, AND VOTING TRENDS

Having thus established a definite connection between religious beliefs and political attitudes, it remains our final task to determine if this connection can offer us insight into the key findings of Chapters 3 and 4: the growing polarization between liberal and conservative Protestants in the 1960s, the sudden movement of Catholics away from the Democrats in 1972, and the decline of the religion effect on presidential voting in 1976. In effect we are now dealing with the last link in the chain of causality that flows from religious beliefs through political attitudes to presidential voting behavior. A vast amount of literature already exists on the topic of how political attitudes affect actual voting behavior and it is not our intention to add directly to this particular area of research. Instead we will draw upon the findings of this literature in an attempt to isolate those political attitudes that seemed to play major roles in affecting the outcome of each of the relevant electoral contests. These findings will then be examined in an attempt to shed light on our ultimate concern: the way that religious beliefs have affected presidential voting behavior in the most recent period of American history.

Although there has been vast disagreement in the literature regarding the magnitude of the impact of policy issues on the electoral decision, a fair amount of consensus has emerged as to which issues played the largest roles in a given election year.[9] This enables us to proceed with our analysis beginning with the 1968 election, which was chosen as a starting point because it was the year in which the polarization between liberal and conservative Protestants reached full force. As the findings of Tables 3.3 and 3.4 indicated, the conservative Protestants were far more likely than the liberals to desert the ranks of the Democratic party. In addition the tables indicated that much of this difference resulted from the impressive conservative Protestant affinity for the candidacy of the third-party candidate, George Wallace. How do we explain these findings? A number of issues have been shown to have played key roles in the election outcome. It has been suggested that the Wallace candidacy in particular was based on an issue-oriented appeal. Most of these issues were also considered to have been important in the 1972 election and therefore were included in the 1972 election survey. However, there is an obvious danger in attempting to apply our 1972 findings to the 1968 election. For this reason we have reexamined the link between issue attitudes and religion for the 1968 survey data. Table 5.14 displays the mean scores for each religious group on a number of key issues for 1968 and compares them to the findings for the analogous questions for 1972. Thus Table 5.14 allows us to do two things: to examine the impact of religious beliefs on issue formation in 1968 and to see if this religious impact underwent any change by 1972.

The most obvious candidate for the role of explaining the voting split between the Protestant groups is the race issue, which by 1968 had taken a number of specific forms. Before examining each of these specific issues, it seems wise to once again begin with a measure of general attitudes toward integration and segregation. The data in Table 5.14 indicate that by 1968 a large gap had developed between the Protestant groups in this regard, with liberals being far more likely to favor integration than the conservatives. Moving on to the specific racial issues, we can see that a somewhat smaller but still important gap had developed between the two groups on the question of government intervention to bring about school integration. But a much more impressive disparity occurred on the race-related issue of how to best handle urban unrest. The years between 1964 and 1968 had seen major riots in a number of urban ghettos throughout the country. In the 1968 campaign both Nixon and Wallace attempted to take advantage of the climate of fear that resulted from these events by stressing the need to reestablish law and order. The data indicate that both of these candidates were able to find a much more sympathetic audience among the conservative Protestants than among members of the liberal Protestant group.

Thus it can be seen that the racial issue in its various forms may provide an important explanation for the voting differences between the Protestant groups in 1968. The special Wallace appeal among conservative Protestants is especially amenable to this type of explanation. It seems useful to mention briefly what issues could not have accounted for these 1968 voting differences. One of these was the Vietnam War issue. The data from Table 5.14 indicate that as of 1968 there was still a great deal of support for American military intervention in Vietnam and that the substantial differences among the religious groups that we found for 1972 had not yet developed. The other issues that could not have accounted for the differences were those that involved an appeal to class self-interest.

TABLE 5.14
Issue Positions for 1968 and 1972

Denominational Category	Year			
	1968		1972	
Integration				
Liberal Protestants	2.58	(185)*	2.28	(276)
Moderate Protestants	2.61	(250)	2.31	(353)
Conservative Protestants	3.12	(139)	3.01	(205)
Catholics	2.27	(226)	2.28	(387)
School Integration				
Liberal Protestants	3.27	(157)	3.41	(232)
Moderate Protestants	3.52	(197)	3.32	(292)
Conservative Protestants	3.66	(119)	3.93	(180)
Catholics	2.81	(190)	3.34	(332)
Job Integration				
Liberal Protestants	3.57	(159)	3.29	(213)
Moderate Protestants	3.28	(212)	3.10	(280)
Conservative Protestants	3.41	(126)	3.61	(173)
Catholics	3.17	(184)	2.90	(301)
Urban Unrest				
Liberal Protestants	3.71	(179)	3.27	(117)
Moderate Protestants	3.99	(245)	3.53	(154)
Conservative Protestants	4.40	(129)	3.65	(89)
Catholics	3.52	(212)	3.10	(174)
Vietnam				
Liberal Protestants	4.38	(181)	3.76	(127)
Moderate Protestants	4.48	(244)	3.77	(173)
Conservative Protestants	4.48	(124)	4.39	(95)
Catholics	4.24	(206)	3.84	(185)

*Figures in parentheses are number of cases.

In our examination of the 1972 data we showed that issues involving government intervention in the job market seemed to evoke such a class-based response, resulting in a virtual neutralization of the religion-based differences between the Protestant groups. Table 5.14 indicates that this was also the case in 1968.

In spite of the removal of the Wallace third-party candidacy the tendency for conservative Protestants to be much more likely than the liberal Protestants to deviate from the normal vote in an anti-Democratic direction continued in 1972. The literature indicates that at least part of the explanation for the maintenance of this gap was the continuing importance of the racial question in 1972. The data from Table 5.14 indicate that the split between liberal and conservative Protestants on the general question of integration actually widened significantly between 1968 and 1972. Evidence of the high salience of racial issues in 1972 comes from examining changes in the mean responses for the two Protestant groups on the question of government intervention to insure fair treatment for blacks in the job market. As suggested earlier this question seems to tap both an economic self-interest and a racial component, resulting in the emergence of both class-based and religion-based effects on attitude formation. In 1968 class seemed to exert the more powerful effect resulting in the fact that liberal Protestants tended to take more conservative stands than conservative Protestants. By 1972 the two groups had reversed positions with the liberal Protestants now emerging as the more liberal of the two on this particular jobs issue. This switch seems to indicate that the issue was now being interpreted more as a racial question than had been the case in 1968, thus increasing the impact of religious beliefs relative to class interests.

However, the racial issues that had played such an important role in dividing the Protestant groups in 1968 were now joined by other religiously divisive issues. One of these was the Vietnam War issue. By 1972 a large gulf had developed between the liberal and conservative Protestants, with the former now being far more likely than the latter to favor a dovish position on the war. Other issues have also been shown to have affected the 1972 election outcome. Many of these may have helped to split the Protestant groups. These other religiously divisive issues included the proper level of military spending and the newly emerging cultural issues of abortion and women's rights.

The second phenomenon we wish to explain by utilizing our findings regarding the effect of religious beliefs on political attitudes is the sudden desertion of Catholics from the Democratic party in 1972. Tables 3.2 and 3.3 showed the fluctuation in the Democratic vote among Catholics from 1960 onward. In both the 1960 and 1964 presidential elections approximately four out of five Catholic voters cast their ballots for the Democratic nominee. In 1968 the Democratic proportion of the Catholic two-party vote dropped to 59 percent. However, the overall drop in Democratic support between 1964 and 1968 did not come disproportionately among Catholics. In fact the drop in Catholic support was actually slightly less than the Democratic decline among liberal Protestants and far less than the decline among conservative Protestants. In addition a significant decline in the Democratic vote could have been expected following the exceptional landslide victory of Lyndon Johnson in 1964.

Far more baffling is the huge drop in the Democratic vote among Catholics between 1968 and 1972. What makes it so baffling is the fact that the Democratic vote among both liberal and conservative Protestants remained virtually unchanged between these two election years. Thus the Democratic loss among Catholics cannot be attributed to general political factors that affected all the groups in the same way. Rather, something must have occurred over this four-year period that impacted more on Catholic voters than on Protestants. What we are trying to explain then is the peculiar rise in the deviation from the normal vote for Catholics relative to the other religious groups. This deviation from the normal vote can, of course, occur in a number of different ways. For instance, it can occur as a result of massive defections of those who identify with one party to the candidate of the other party. Alternatively, it can result from the disproportionate appeal of one's party candidate among those who consider themselves to be Independents.

Table 5.15 gives us a clearer indication of the kind of changes that occurred between 1968 and 1972 by displaying the voting patterns of each religious group while controlling for party identification. Certain new facts now come to light if we compare the voting patterns of Catholics and liberal Protestants for the two years. In 1968 Catholics deviated from the normal vote in the Republican direction at a considerably lower rate than the liberal Protestants. This relative success of the Humphrey campaign among Catholics resulted primarily from the Democratic nominee's

TABLE 5.15
Religion by Vote by Party Identification for 1968 and 1972
(in percentages)

	Vote		
Denominational Category	Humphrey	Nixon	Wallace
1968			
Democratic			
Liberal Protestants	68	18	14
Moderate Protestants	61	28	11
Conservative Protestants	39	25	36
Catholics	75	18	7
n of cases	334		
Independent			
Liberal Protestants	12	78	10
Moderate Protestants	21	64	15
ConservativeProtestants	9	54	37
Catholics	43	48	9
n of cases	240		
Republican			
Liberal Protestants	4	94	1
Moderate Protestants	3	91	6
Conservative Protestants	4	85	11
Catholics	11	82	7
n of cases	250		

Denominational Category	Vote	
	McGovern	Nixon
	1972	
	Democratic	
Liberal Protestants	53	47
Moderate Protestants	50	50
Conservative Protestants	33	67
Catholics	53	47
n of cases	477	
	Independent	
Liberal Protestants	34	66
Moderate Protestants	27	73
Conservative Protestants	14	86
Catholics	30	70
n of cases	378	
	Republican	
Liberal Protestants	6	94
Moderate Protestants	4	96
Conservative Protestants	3	97
Catholics	9	91
n of cases	397	

differential appeal among Independents. Among Democratic identifiers Humphrey did only slightly better among Catholics than
among liberal Protestants. However, among Independents Humphrey
received only 12 percent of the liberal Protestant vote as opposed
to 43 percent of the Catholic vote.

In 1972 the two groups reversed themselves. In this year the
deviation from the normal vote in the Republican direction was
far greater among Catholics than among liberal Protestants. Table
5.15 tells us how this switch came about. A huge drop in Democratic
support among Catholics occurred among Democratic identifiers
over the four-year period, while a smaller but still impressive drop
occurred among Catholic Independents. Among liberal Protestants
McGovern actually did considerably better than Humphrey among
Independents, though considerably worse than his predecessor
among Democrats. The result of all this was that in 1972 Catholic
and liberal Protestant voting patterns were virtually identical among
each of the partisan groups. The greater deviation from the normal
vote among Catholics resulted mainly from the fact that the expected Democratic vote was much higher for this group than it
was for the latter group.

All of this is important because it tells us exactly what it
is that needs explaining. In 1968 Catholics of all partisan persuasions
were more likely than the analogous liberal Protestant groups to
vote Democratic. This fact is consistent with our issue findings
for 1968. On each of the issues we examined, Catholics tended to
be somewhat more liberal than the liberal Protestants. By 1972
the voting patterns of Catholics and liberal Protestants among
all partisan groups had essentially equalized. This equalization, of
course, occurred largely as a result of the massive drop in Democratic support among Catholics. But the important point is that
this drop in Catholic support need not have been a result of factors
completely unique to members of this group. In other words, we
need not look for a "Catholic" issue or issues that Richard Nixon
took advantage of in 1972. In fact only one such possible "Catholic"
issue is indicated by our previous issue analysis for 1972: the conflict
over the legalization of abortion. This is the only issue on which
Catholics were substantially more conservative than liberal Protestants in this election year. Although the literature suggests that the
abortion issue may have played a role in the 1972 election outcome,
it is doubtful that it in itself can explain the massive Catholic defections from the Democratic party.

What other issues could possibly have caused so many Catholics to switch votes over these four years? The findings of Table 5.15 are extremely useful here because they tell us the kinds of issues that could provide us with an explanation. These findings indicate that Catholics and liberal Protestants were equally supportive of the Democratic nominee, and that each of these groups was far more pro-McGovern than the conservative Protestants. This pattern could have resulted from any issues on which both Catholics and liberal Protestants were substantially more liberal than members of the conservative Protestant group. Included among the issues that fit this description are many that have been mentioned in the voting literature as having played significant roles in affecting the 1972 election outcome. By 1972 liberal Protestants had become as liberal as Catholics on the basic question of integration. In addition both of these groups had become more dovish on Vietnam. On each of these issues the two groups had become far more liberal than the conservative Protestants. Similar patterns occurred for responses to the questions concerning aid to minorities and military spending. On the basis of our findings as to how the various religious groups divided up on each of these issues, it is easy to understand why among each partisan group Catholics and liberal Protestants were far more likely than conservative Protestants to support the candidacy of George McGovern. The real mystery is why McGovern's support was so weak even among these former two groups. There are two possible explanations for this phenomenon. One is the existence of a highly salient issue that we have not discussed on which both of these groups were quite conservative. In fact such an issue did exist in 1972: busing to achieve school integration. On this issue, which is believed to have played an important role in the election outcome, an antibusing consensus existed among all of the religious groups. Still, this one issue does not adequately explain the Nixon landslide. But there is a second explanation for the lack of McGovern support among even the more liberal religious groups. This second factor has to do with the way that individuals use their own issue positions in deciding how to cast their votes. Logically, if one wishes to vote on the basis of the issues he must examine the issue positions of the candidates and decide which candidate's stands are more in agreement with his own. He then must cast his ballot for that particular candidate. What this tells us is that issue voting is dependent both on the issue positions of potential voters and the perceived issue positions of the major party candidates. Much of the voting literature on the 1972 election suggests that George McGovern was badly defeated not because the country had moved farther to the right but rather because he was perceived as too far to the left.[10] The result was that many normally Democratic voters found themselves more in issue agreement with Nixon than with McGovern. This suggestion is very much in agreement with our findings. While Nixon may have been able to score points on the newly emerging issues of busing and abortion, our overall issue analysis indicates that there was little reason to have expected the Democrats to lose ground between 1968 and 1972. In fact on the important issues of Vietnam and race, by 1972 a kind of liberal alliance had emerged between Catholics and liberal Protestants (with liberal Protestants moving farther left to join the Catholics on the racial question and both groups moving left on Vietnam). Thus the loss of Democratic support among both of these groups—especially among the Catholics—seems to tell us more about the failures of the McGovern candidacy than about mass-level changes in political attitudes.

In short the massive drop in Catholic support for the Democratic party in presidential elections over the four-year period between 1968 and 1972 seems to have been a result of changes at the party's elite level. It was not so much that the Catholics had become too conservative for the Democrats as it was that the Democrats had become too liberal for the Catholics.

This leaves us with one final event that still needs explaining. This is the apparent decline of the religion effect in 1976, following two elections in which religion seemed to play a powerful role in affecting the voting outcome. There are a number of possible explanations for this decline in the link between religious beliefs and voting behavior. As our previous analysis has implied, such a decline must have involved some kind of change in the way that political attitudes mediate between religious beliefs and the voting decision. This change could have resulted from two different kinds of events. The first possibility is that the political conflicts that had led many individuals to choose sides largely on the basis of their religious beliefs had been resolved by 1976. For instance, a genuine decline in racial tensions based on the success of the civil rights movement would have resulted in a decrease in the political divisions between the various religious groups. American political history offers numerous examples of issues on which intense conflict eventually gave way to overwhelming consensus. To the extent that such issues are related to religious beliefs, this sort of issue evolution can help account for the rise and fall of the influence of religion on the vote.

The findings of Table 5.16, which compares issue positions of each religious group for 1972 and 1976, offer some support for this sort of explanation. The data indicate that over this four-year period attitude differences among the religious groups declined sharply on the issues of general integration, school integration, minority aid, military spending, and urban unrest. All of this is in addition to the fact that the religiously divisive Vietnam War issue had completely dropped out of the picture. It is possible then that the 1976 election may have occurred in a period in which there were simply no important conflicts in society on which the various religious groups could have been expected to take opposing stands.

However, the findings of Table 5.16 are also consistent with a second explanation for the decline of the religion effect in the 1976 election. This latter explanation puts much more emphasis than the former on elite political behavior. According to this view the formation of issue attitudes among the mass public is highly dependent on the way that issues are defined by highly visible political elites, especially the presidential nominees of the major political parties. If candidates fail to take clear issue stands, the result will be a low level of issue salience, issue consistency, and issue voting.[11] There is widespread agreement that such issue clarity was greatly lacking in the 1976 presidential campaign, while there is evidence that fairly high levels of issue clarity existed in both the 1968 and 1972 races. If this was in fact the case the expected result would have been a drop in mass issue consistency and issue voting between 1972 and 1976, something the literature seems to confirm.[12]

Earlier on we suggested that for most individuals political attitudes exist only on the periphery of their overall psychological structures. We can expect that this fact will be all the more true during periods of low issue salience. The more peripheral these political attitudes are, the less likely they are to be influenced by the more central elements in these psychological structures such as strongly held religious beliefs. Therefore the decline in issue salience between 1972 and 1976 could have been expected to result in a reduction in the influence of religious beliefs on issue

TABLE 5.16
Issue Positions for 1972 and 1976

Denominational Category	Year			
	1972		*1976*	
Integration				
Liberal Protestants	2.28	(276)	2.24	(246)
Moderate Protestants	2.31	(353)	2.40	(361)
Conservative Protestants	3.01	(205)	2.66	(233)
Catholics	2.28	(387)	2.39	(382)
School Integration				
Liberal Protestants	3.41	(232)	3.99	(161)
Moderate Protestants	3.32	(292)	3.70	(236)
Conservative Protestants	3.93	(180)	4.07	(153)
Catholics	3.34	(332)	3.78	(258)
Busing				
Liberal Protestants	6.32	(263)	6.16	(228)
Moderate Protestants	6.50	(335)	6.31	(346)
Conservative Protestants	6.67	(204)	6.60	(226)
Catholics	6.43	(377)	6.41	(363)
Minority Aid				
Liberal Protestants	4.28	(248)	4.56	(227)
Moderate Protestants	4.55	(317)	4.55	(322)
Conservative Protestants	4.93	(192)	4.63	(203)
Catholics	4.24	(367)	4.50	(354)
Military Spending				
Liberal Protestants	3.30	(139)	4.30	(246)
Moderate Protestants	3.63	(167)	4.42	(367)
Conservative Protestants	4.02	(102)	4.52	(227)
Catholics	3.33	(194)	4.40	(385)
Urban Unrest				
Liberal Protestants	3.27	(117)	3.47	(222)
Moderate Protestants	3.53	(154)	3.42	(276)
Conservative Protestants	3.65	(89)	3.59	(170)
Catholics	3.10	(174)	3.18	(331)
Abortion				
Liberal Protestants	2.80	(276)	2.96	(241)
Moderate Protestants	2.73	(354)	2.72	(370)
Conservative Protestants	2.30	(207)	2.36	(231)
Catholics	2.33	(383)	2.25	(377)

attitude formation. The ultimate result would have been the lessening of differences among religious groups in terms of issue attitudes and therefore in terms of the vote. Thus the data in Table 5.16 offer evidence to support this second explanation as well.

How then can we determine which of the two different explanations for the decline of the religion effect is the correct one? The answer is that only time will tell. The rise and fall of political issues is a complex phenomenon, undoubtedly involving aspects of both mass-level and elite-level change. Some issues that played important roles in the 1972 election had disappeared by 1976, never to return again. An obvious example is the Vietnam War issue. Other religiously divisive issues such as those related to racial conflict may have simply gone into dormancy, waiting to be resurrected by future candidates willing to take clear and opposing stands on them.[13] Only the occurrence of future elections can tell us if any of the important issues of 1968 and 1972 fall into this latter category.[14] If they do they undoubtedly will be joined by new issues, some of which will call into play deeply held religious beliefs. Thus the impact of religion on voting behavior is not likely to disappear permanently. As long as there is religion, politics will never be far from its grasp.

THE ISSUE CONNECTION

Thus far the evidence we have presented strongly suggests that the differences in voting patterns found among religious groups in recent presidential elections were indeed rooted in new religion-related issues that found their way onto the political agenda. However, it can be argued that what is needed is a more direct test of the notion that religious beliefs affect presidential voting behavior by first influencing the development of attitudes toward key political issues of the day. Such a test can be accomplished by examining the relationship between religion and the vote while controlling for issue attitudes. Unless our theoretical notions have been far off the mark, such issue controls should result in a significant reduction in the impact of religion on the vote. Specifically, when we hold issue attitudes constant most of the differences we have found among the major religious groups in terms of their deviations from the normal vote should disappear.

Since our main focus has been the 1972 election, it makes sense to apply our issue controls for that year. Our previous analysis suggested that the religion-related issues that could have accounted for the voting differences among religious groups in 1972 included civil rights issues, moral issues such as abortion and women's rights, and foreign policy issues such as Vietnam and military spending. In the way of accomplishing our task more efficiently, whenever possible we have combined individual issue items into more general issue indexes.[15] Table 5.17 displays the voting patterns of each of the religious groups when controls for these issue items and issue indexes are instituted. Of greatest concern to us is how these controls affect the differences between religious groups in terms of their deviation from the normal vote. For the sake of convenience, these effects are summarized in Table 5.18.[16]

Our previous analysis suggested that one major reason for the differences in religious group voting patterns found in 1972 was the high salience of civil rights issues in that election year. On such issues both Catholics and liberal Protestants were found to be significantly more likely than conservative Protestants to adopt liberal or pro-civil rights stands. This could account for at least part of the tendency for the conservative Protestants to be more likely than the others to deviate from the normal vote in the Republican direction. Such a conclusion seems to be borne out by the findings of Table 5.18. When controls are instituted for the civil rights issue index, the voting gap between liberal and conservative Protestants is reduced from 24 percentage points to 16 points, a reduction of 33 percent of the total. The difference between conservative Protestants and Catholics is reduced from 10 to 2 percentage points, a reduction of 80 percent of the total. Thus it seems rather likely that the religion-related civil rights issues of 1972 played a major role in bringing about the political polarization of religious groups in that year.

Our previous analysis also suggested that a similar role was played by the salient foreign policy issues of the 1972 election year. It has been shown that on both the issues of Vietnam and military spending the conservative Protestants stood out for their relatively hard-line stands. The important role that these two foreign policy issues played in polarizing the three religious groups is also confirmed by the findings of Table 5.18. When controls are applied for the Vietnam War issue, the deviation gap between liberal and conservative Protestants is reduced from 24 to 15 percentage points,

TABLE 5.17
Vote by Religion by Issue, 1972

	Issue Category					
	Left		Center		Right	
Denominational Category	Percent Democratic	Dev.	Percent Democratic	Dev.	Percent Democratic	Dev.
Civil Rights Index						
Liberal Protestants	43	−2	20	−18	19	−24
Moderate Protestants	38	−8	15	−26	19	−23
Conservative Protestants	47	−6	26	−35	13	−46
Catholics	53	−19	39	−28	27	−39
n of cases	241		345		434	
Moral Index						
Liberal Protestants	39	−5	19	−19	28	−15
Moderate Protestants	33	−10	20	−22	23	−23
Conservative Protestants	26	−37	18	−35	19	−43
Catholics	38	−28	44	−25	31	−37
n of cases	247		484		448	
Vietnam						
Liberal Protestants	56	−3	18	−25	0	−26
Moderate Protestants	46	−3	21	−25	0	−36
Conservative Protestants	36	−21	15	−39	15	−41
Catholics	61	−6	36	−29	19	−41
n of cases	145		318		118	
Guarantee Jobs						
Liberal Protestants	67	+10	29	−8	20	−17
Moderate Protestants	63	−6	23	−16	10	−35
Conservative Protestants	44	−29	24	−30	12	−55
Catholics	50	−24	39	−35	28	−37
n of cases	83		322		175	
Military Spending						
Liberal Protestants	44	+1			17	−15
Moderate Protestants	38	−11			19	−25
Conservative Protestants	52	−12			14	−47
Catholics	62	−14			20	−47
n of cases	223				383	

a reduction of 38 percent of the total. Applying controls for the military spending issue reduces the difference between Catholics and conservative Protestants by 100 percent of the total. Taken together these two foreign policy issues do indeed seem to account for a large portion of the voting differences between the conservative Protestants and the two more liberal religious groups.

Finally, we suggested that the newly emerging moral issues of abortion and women's rights may have played a role in dividing the religious groups in 1972. For this reason it comes as somewhat of a surprise to find that when controls are instituted for our moral issues index no significant changes occur in group voting differences. Similar results occur when controls are instituted for the two issues separately. The data in Table 5.17 provide us with a clue as to why this is the case. The lack of variation in voting behavior across issue categories suggests that these moral issues never attained the level of salience needed to affect the voting decisions of significant numbers of voters. In short, in the context of the 1972 presidential election these issues really didn't matter very much.[17]

Nevertheless, the findings of Tables 5.17 and 5.18 provide us with strong evidence in support of our overall model. In 1972 religious beliefs managed to influence the voting decisions of large numbers of voters by first influencing their attitudes toward civil rights and foreign policy issues. The relatively conservative stands taken by conservative Protestants on these issues seem to account for their greater tendency to deviate from the normal vote in the Republican direction than either the Catholics or the liberal Protestants. While offering confirmation of our model, these latest findings have also provided us the chance to better understand some of the group voting trends discussed earlier. Specifically, we now have more concrete evidence as to the kinds of issues that helped to polarize the two major Protestant groups in the late 1960s and early 1970s.

But do these findings also offer us any insight into the behavior of Catholic voters in 1972? As we have seen, one of the major factors contributing to the landslide Democratic defeat in the 1972 presidential election was the startling decline in Catholic support. In 1968 Hubert Humphrey had nearly won the presidency with the support of a majority of Catholic voters. But by 1972 this support had slipped to a point at which Catholics of all partisan persuasions were no more likely than liberal Protestants to vote for the Democratic candidate. This fact hinted at the rise of religion-related issues on which Catholics and liberal Protestants were equally likely to take liberal stands. We can now say with greater certainty that we have identified such issues: civil rights and the foreign policy issues of Vietnam and military spending. As these issues rose in importance they replaced the more class-based issues that had separated Catholics and liberal Protestants in previous election years. A new party system, based more on the religious divisions in American society, came temporarily into play. There was nothing about this system that necessarily precluded the possibility of a Democratic victory in the 1972 presidential race. In theory the Democrats could have put together a new majority coalition, centered around Catholics and enough liberal Protestants to replace conservative Protestant defectors. The fact that this did not happen is a function of the specific political events of that election year. As it was, the perception of George McGovern as being too radical managed to drive away millions of potential Democratic voters and insure the landslide victory of his Republican opponent. But the fact remains that under the right circumstances religious beliefs can come to play a critically important role in determining the outcome of a given presidential race. It is this most basic finding that has major implications for the future of the American political system.

Still, this part of our analysis might seem incomplete if we failed to say something about the controversial 1980 presidential race. Our examination of religious voting in Chapter 3 provided hard

TABLE 5.18
Group Differences in Deviation from the Normal Vote (1972)
(in percentages)

	Group Differences		
Controlling for	Liberal Protestant/ Conservative Protestant	Catholic/ Conservative Protestant	Catholic/ Liberal Protestant
Civil rights index	16	2	14
Moral index	24	8	16
Vietnam	15	9	6
Military spending	25	0	26
Guarantee jobs	29	3	26
No controls	24	10	14

evidence to refute the claims made by religious right leaders that they were in large part responsible for the impressive victory of Ronald Reagan. The type of issue analysis we have undertaken in this section provides us with yet another way to look at this controversy. If, in spite of our claims, religious beliefs really did matter in 1980 there must have existed religion-related issues that were salient enough to affect the voting decisions of large numbers of voters. What possible issues that arose during the course of the 1980 presidential campaign could have fulfilled this requirement?

Two such possible issues include the conflict over school prayer and the debate surrounding the. proposed Equal Rights Amendment. We have already shown that on both of these issues religious beliefs seemed to influence the attitudes of many voters. In addition, Ronald Reagan's clear-cut stands in favor of organized school prayer and against the ERA put him in definite opposition to Jimmy Carter and the dominant leadership of the Democratic party. Thus both of these issues had the potential to bring religion into the national political picture. In order to determine whether this potential was realized we have examined the impact of religion on the vote while controlling for each of these issues. The results of these controls are displayed in Tables 5.19 and 5.20.

Another possible religion-related issue in 1980 was foreign policy. In Tables 5.19 and 5.20 we have also provided controls for a 1980 issue question that attempted to measure a respondent's attitude toward the Soviet Union. This question was used to divide respondents on the basis of their relative distrust of the Soviets and of efforts to reach political accommodations with them. This sort of hawk-dove question is exactly the type of foreign policy question we could expect to divide voters along religious lines. It is also another issue on which the position of Ronald Reagan could easily be discerned, given the fact that he spent the better part of his political career building a reputation as an anti-Soviet hard-liner.[18]

Thus all three issues provided potential sources of religious division in the 1980 presidential race, but the findings of Table 5.19 indicate that this potential was never realized. The lack of a significant and consistent variation in voting patterns across issue categories on all three issues suggests that they never achieved the level of salience needed to make a real difference in the election outcome. In short these religion-related issues were simply not important enough to divide voters along religious lines. This conclusion is bolstered by the findings of Table 5.20. Controlling for these issues has virtually no impact on the very small religious effect that was found for 1980. Eliminating these issues does not change the voting behavior of the major American religious groups relative to one another.

In sum, we have been unable to uncover any evidence that religion-related issues had a significant impact on the 1980 presidential race. Thus there is all the more reason to doubt that the important victory of Ronald Reagan in 1980 had its roots in the deeply held religious beliefs of the American public.

TABLE 5.19
Vote by Religion by Issue, 1980

| | Issue Category | | | | | |
| | Left | | Center | | Right | |
Denominational Category	Percent Democrat	Dev.	Percent Democrat	Dev.	Percent Democrat	Dev.
	School Prayer					
Liberal Protestants	55	−2	44	+11	32	−13
Moderate Protestants	47	−12	25	−25	24	−18
Conservative Protestants	33	−17	0	−25	44	−16
Catholics	58	−10	57	+7	44	−17
n of cases	96		22		427	
	ERA					
Liberal Protestants	45	−6			25	−11
Moderate Protestants	40	−13			17	−25
Conservative Protestants	64	−13			23	−23
Catholics	50	−15			27	−25
n of cases	286				278	
	Russia					
Liberal Protestants	42	−7	32	−2	29	−15
Moderate Protestants	37	−11	31	−13	14	−31
Conservative Protestants	48	−14	41	−25	33	−18
Catholics	53	−5	43	−18	32	−25
n of cases	220		133		217	

TABLE 5.20
Group Differences in Deviation From the Normal Vote, (1980)
(in percentages)

	Group differences		
Controlling for	*Liberal Protestant/ Conservative Protestant*	*Catholic/ Conservative Protestant*	*Catholic/ Liberal Protestant*
School prayer	6	−2*	5
ERA	9	2	11
Russia	9	−2	7
No controls	8	1	9

*A minus sign indicates that when controls are applied the two groups reverse positions relative to one another, in terms of deviation from the normal vote.

NOTES

1. The view that voting behavior is most directly affected by political attitudes concerning the candidates and issues and that other factors lie farther back in the funnel of causality was first set forth in Angus Campbell, Philip E. Converse, Warren E. Miller, and Donald E. Stokes, *The American Voter* (New York: John Wiley, 1960). In keeping with this model we are suggesting here that religious beliefs affect voting behavior through their influence on the development of these political attitudes. It is also possible that religious beliefs exercise a more indirect effect by playing a role in the development of partisan identification. This possibility will be examined in Chapter 7. For a discussion of the concept of centrality and its relevance to the development of political attitudes see Philip E. Converse, "The Nature of Belief Systems in Mass Publics," in David Apter, *Ideology and Discontent* (New York: The Free Press, 1964), p. 208.

2. Norman H. Nie, Sydney Verba, and John R. Petrocik, *The Changing American Voter* (Cambridge, Mass.: Harvard University Press, 1979).

3. As suggested above the political stimuli to which potential voters are exposed will be highly dependent on elite-level change, especially the behavior of the presidential nominees of the major political parties. Evidence of the important difference that this can make in the relationship between religion and the vote was provided in Chapter 4. However, changes in politically relevant stimuli may also occur as a result of mass-level change in society. The historical evidence presented in Chapter 1 suggested that this was especially true in certain political periods. In Chapter 6 we will attempt to determine if this more episodic explanation for the rise and fall of the religion affect can offer us any insight into the nature of contemporary political events.

4. It seems worthwhile to discuss here exactly what constitutes a theoretically significant difference in group mean responses to any of the issue questions. A number of things must be considered. The most obvious is the overall size of the issue index. A difference of a half a point between groups is much more meaningful when the maximum theoretical difference is 4 points than when it is 12 points. In order to show the maximum theoretical difference for each issue question we have displayed all of the possible responses for each issue in the relevant issue table. Second, we must consider the fact that on many issues there is a tendency for respondents to cluster around the middle position. This, of course, tends to minimize differences in group means and therefore makes those differences that do occur all the more impressive. Finally, it is important to consider the overall issue picture. Our ultimate concern is explaining voting behavior. Therefore, consistency across issues is critical. If the various religious groups tend to occupy the same positions relative to one another across most of the issues, then it becomes much more possible to explain the voting patterns that we have uncovered in previous chapters. This is, in fact, the case as Catholics and liberal Protestants turn out to be more liberal than conservative Protestants on virtually every issue. We have not dwelled on statistical significance because the large number of cases makes statistical significance rather easy to achieve. However, for the sake of completeness, statistically significant differences between the conservative Protestants and the two liberal religious groups in the overall population are indicated in the issue tables.

5. It is possible that denominational affiliation itself may have an effect on one's perception of his own social class standing, independent of income. In order to test for this possibility we have examined the relationship between subjective social class and religious denomination for 1972. The data confirm that even within the broad income categories liberal Protestants tended to rate their own social class standing higher than Catholics. This suggests the possibility that the differences between Catholics and liberal Protestants on issues related to job-market concerns may have been a result of disparities between them in subjective social class.

6. This is not to say that issues that are more class related will necessarily dominate issues that are based largely on religious belief when it comes to affecting the voting decision. The question of which issues or issue cleavages will dominate at a given point in time is a more difficult one to answer, although a critically important one for those who wish to understand the workings of democratic political systems. All that is being suggested here is that the way that the issue is defined will largely determine whether class or religion is more important in the formation of public attitudes on it.

7. It should be pointed out here that the use of questions from the 1980 survey could bias the results against the confirmation of our hypotheses relating religious beliefs and issue attitudes. This is because the voting data discussed in Chapter 3 seem to indicate that religion played relatively little role in the 1980 voting outcome. This fact in turn may have been the result of a lack of salient religion-related issues. This sort of lack of issue salience could be expected to lessen the impact of religious beliefs on issue attitude formation. Therefore, any religious group issue differences found for this year would seem to be all the more impressive.

8. It should be mentioned here that a national survey conducted by the Associated Press and NBC News in January 1982 attempted to distinguish between the moral and legal questions surrounding abortion. The results showed that among those who believed abortion to be wrong, Catholics were slightly more likely than Protestants (taken as a whole) to say abortion should be legal. This finding is reported in the *Miami Herald*, Thursday, February 4, 1982. Given the seriousness of the issue for Catholics, this finding would seem to be added testimony to the general tendency of Catholics to reject state intervention in the area of morality.

9. These findings regarding the role of issues in the 1968, 1972, and 1976 elections are drawn from the following works: Philip E. Converse, Warren E. Miller, Jerrald G. Rusk, and Arthur C. Wolfe, "Continuity and Change in American Politics: Parties and Issues in the 1968 Election," *American Political Science Review* 63 (December 1969): 1083-1105; Arthur H. Miller, Warren E. Miller, Alden S. Raine, and Thad A. Brown, "A Majority Party in Disarray: Policy Polarization in the 1972 Election," *American Political Science Review* 70 (September 1976): 753-78; Warren Miller and Arthur Miller, "Issues, Candidates, and Partisan Divisions in the 1972 Presidential Election," *British Journal of Political Science* 5 (October 1975): 394-434; Arthur Miller, "Partisanship Reinstated? A Comparison of the 1972 and 1976 U.S. Presidential Elections," *British Journal of Political Science* 8 (April 1978): 129-53; and Nie, Verba, and Petrocik.

10. This suggestion that the leftward movement of the electorate on many issues between 1968 and 1972 was more than offset by McGovern's perceived radicalism is made in Miller, Miller, Raine, and Brown. A similar idea, that McGovern failed to capture much of his natural liberal constituency, is expressed in Warren E. Miller and Teresa E. Levitin, *Leadership and Change: Presidential Elections from 1952 to 1976* (Cambridge, Mass.: Winthrop, 1976).

11. The best argument for this point of view is made in Nie, Verba, and Petrocik.

12. Ibid.

13. Actually, evidence that many such religiously divisive issues had not been resolved by 1976 is contained in the findings of Chapter 4. In this chapter we were able to show that different combinations of candidates in 1976 would have resulted in vast increases in the effect of religion on the vote. This seems to imply that important issues related to religious beliefs were in fact only lying dormant, able to be brought to the forefront by candidates who had histories of taking relatively clear stands on them.

14. As we have seen in Chapter 3, there seems to have been relatively little religion effect in 1980. We have not attempted to determine if this resulted from a low-issue election or an election in which the important issues were unrelated to religious beliefs.

15. The individual issue items taken from the 1972 data set include the questions on abortion, women's equality, Vietnam, military spending, general integration, and school integration. Each of these individual issue items was then recoded so that they contained no more than three issue categories. Next, the indexes were formed. The individual items on abortion and women's equality were combined into our moral index. The individual items on general

integration and school integration were combined into our civil rights index. Finally, both indexes were trichotomized to make them easier to use.

16.   The summaries in Table 5.18 were formed by taking the weighted mean average difference between religious groups, across issue categories. By difference, of course, we mean the difference between religious groups in terms of their deviation from the normal vote.

17.   We have maintained that the guaranteed jobs issue of 1972 was one that tapped heavily into the class dimension. This notion seems to be borne out by the data in Table 5.18. Controlling for this issue increases the liberalism of the liberal Protestants relative to the other religious groups. This was to be expected since the higher economic status of liberal Protestants causes them to be pulled in the conservative direction on this issue. Therefore removing it makes them relatively more liberal.

18.   The two 1980 tables were formed in the same manner as those for 1972. For the Russia issue the question reads as follows: "Some people feel it is important for us to try very hard to get along with Russia. Others feel it is a big mistake to try too hard to get along with Russia. Where would you place yourself on this scale or haven't you thought much about this?"

6

Religion and
Mass-Level Change

INTRODUCTION

The previous chapters in our study succeeded in accomplishing many of our analytical goals. First we were able to show that the members of the major religious denominations in America differ significantly along a number of religious belief dimensions. Next we offered strong evidence that these religious belief differences played a major role in affecting voting behavior in a number of recent presidential elections. Finally evidence was shown to suggest that these religious beliefs affect voting behavior by first affecting the development of attitudes toward many of the major political issues of the day.

It is our contention at this point that the evidence linking religious beliefs and presidential voting behavior is quite strong. However, along the way toward making this case we have also begun to address a somewhat different research question. In the process of establishing the link between religious beliefs and voting behavior we have provided rather clear evidence that the magnitude of this linkage varies greatly over time. Why exactly is this relationship subject to such enormous variation? In Chapter 4 we provided what seems to be at least a partial answer to this question. A great deal of the variation in the magnitude of the impact of religious beliefs on presidential voting seems to result from the changing nature of the presidential nominees from one election to the next. In short it can be said that various combinations of presidential candidates are not equally likely to lead voters to choose sides on the basis of their religious beliefs. This particular explanation for religious-political change was originally derived from the brief historical analysis undertaken in Chapter 1. Because of this it was particularly gratifying that this proposition could be largely confirmed through the use of survey data from the most recent presidential election studies.

This historical analysis also led us to develop a second explanation for religious-political change. While the former explanation focuses on changes at the elite level of politics, this latter proposition places emphasis on the ways that changes occurring at the mass level of society can impact on the relationship between religious beliefs and political behavior. Specifically, it was suggested that at certain points in time one or another religious group may begin to feel a decline in its relative social status as a result of economic, social, or demographic trends. When this happens such a group is likely to strike out in defense of its former status position. During such periods the temptation to use government as an instrument for achieving religious ends will be greatly increased. Thus it may be accurate to speak in terms of periodic occurrences of heightened activity along the religious-political front. Because of the nature of mass-level social change, it is likely that these periods will be of longer duration than a single election campaign. Therefore this second proposition concerns itself with a type of change that is likely to be slower to develop than that brought about by the regular turnover of the major party presidential nominees.

The usefulness of such a mass-level periodic explanation for understanding modern presidential politics can be called into question. In our analysis we have examined the six most recent presidential elections. This analysis has shown that the magnitude of the religious impact has varied greatly from one election to the next. There is little evidence of any long-term trends in one direction or another. In short the presidential voting data from 1960 through 1980 seem to be incompatible with any sort of periodic explanation of religious-political change.

However, this does not mean that a periodic explanation for this sort of political change is totally without merit. The historical data seem to indicate that there are indeed such periods of heightened religious influence in the political realm. It may be that the election series that we have examined happened to fall outside of such a period. Yet there is some reason to believe that a periodic upturn may now be upon us. The recent stirrings of the so-called religious right have been well publicized. These stirrings have included substantial organizational and fund-raising activities and, though there is evidence that their impact on the 1980 presidential election was of minimal importance, the religious right may yet emerge as a powerful influence on American politics.

How do we explain this apparent upsurge in the political activity of conservative religious groups? A great deal of it may simply be the result of strategic decisions made by leading conservative political figures.[1] Yet it is also possible that something more is happening. On the surface at least, this most recent upturn in the political activity of the religious right greatly resembles analogous movements in the past. It is our task in this chapter to see if the ideas developed in Chapter 1 can be used to help explain this most recent political phenomenon. Certain things are immediately obvious. In the first place the religious groups that are currently on the political attack fall mainly on the conservative end of the Protestant spectrum, a fact that is quite consistent with the usual historical pattern. Other characteristics of the new movement, such as its heavy moral flavor and its attacks on societal change, are also consistent with the pattern laid out in Chapter 1. Yet for our model to fit the current period something else must be present. This final component is the presence of genuine feelings of status threat among a significant proportion of American conservative Protestants. Without this final component the modern movement is not likely ever to reach the strength and endurance achieved by the analogous movements of the past. Therefore by testing for the presence of feelings of status displacement we will be in a better position not only to understand what has happened thus far but also to predict what is likely to occur in years to come.

MEASURING STATUS DISPLACEMENT

In Chapter 1 it was pointed out that two rather distinct definitions of status and status displacement have emerged in the sociological literature on status politics. Used in the first sense, status refers to social prestige and status politics to the kinds of social conflict that flow out of changes in the relative prestige rankings of various societal groups. This sort of status threat can result from changes in a group's economic, educational, or demographic standing.

Applied to the present situation the question can be formulated in more precise terms. Does the apparent increase in the political activity of the conservative Protestants result from feelings of loss of social prestige due to some sort of social class or demographic decline relative to other religious groups?

Fortunately this question can be answered by examining the relevant survey data at hand, which do not deal directly with the question of perceived social prestige. However, the data can be used to determine if the conservative Protestants have in fact undergone some sort of objective decline along these lines. If it can be shown that such an objective decline has not taken place, this sort of social prestige explanation for the recent upsurge in political activity among conservative Protestants probably can be rejected with a fair degree of certainty.

In order to test for the occurrence of such objective social changes we have examined the social characteristics of each religious group at two points in time, 1960 and 1980. The social variables with which we are concerned include group percentage of the overall population, income, and education. Table 6.1 displays the breakdown of each religious category on the first of these variables, group percentage of the overall population. Although it would be incorrect to claim that group size is perfectly correlated with group prestige,

TABLE 6.1
A Religious Profile of Americans, 1960-80
(in percentages)

	Year	
Denominational Category	*1960*	*1980*
Liberal Protestants	25	18
Moderate Protestants	27	23
Conservative Protestants	14	16
Catholics	23	25
Jews	4	3
Others	7	16
n of cases	1,346	848

Source: All of the tables in this chapter were compiled by the author.

it is probably fair to say that members of a group that is decreasing as a percentage of the population may well find their situation to be socially precarious. In this regard it is interesting to note that a fair amount of change did occur between 1960 and 1980 in the relative sizes of some of the religious groups. Yet these trends did not adversely affect the demographic standing of the conservative Protestants. In fact the data offer some evidence that both the conservative Protestants and the Catholics increased slightly as a percentage of the total population over this 20-year period. The only group to lose significant demographic ground was the liberal Protestants. These findings are consistent with the age distributions discussed in Chapter 2, which showed that both Catholics and conservative Protestants tended to be younger than the liberal Protestants, a consequence perhaps of differences in birth rates among members of these three religious groups. The only religious category to increase really significantly in size over this period was the "Others" category, the result mainly of an increased tendency of respondents to fail to give any religious preference at all.

Table 6.2 displays the breakdown of the four major religious groups by income at the two points in time. The specific cutoff points were chosen in an attempt to divide each sample as evenly as possible into three separate income categories. The vast change in the average income over this period makes comparisons between years somewhat difficult. Nevertheless, the data do allow us to get some sense of how the various religious groups fared relative to one another. It can be seen that as of 1960 the conservative Protestants were clearly the poorest of the religious groups.[2] By 1980 the income gaps between this group and each of the other three religious groups had actually declined significantly. Thus, as was the case with Table 6.1, there is nothing in these data to indicate an unfavorable social trend that could have resulted in a loss of social prestige among members of the conservative Protestant group.

Finally, Table 6.3 displays the breakdown of the four religious groups by education for each of the two years. In this case the respondents were divided into three categories, including those with no more than a grade school education, those with at least some high school, and those with at least some college. It can be readily seen that the educational levels of all of the religious groups increased greatly from 1960 to 1980. There were, however, some

TABLE 6.2
Religion by Income, 1960-80
(in percentages)

	Income Category		
Denominational Category	Up to $3,999	$4,000 to $5,999	$6,000 and over
1960			
Liberal Protestants	29	24	47
Moderate Protestants	27	29	44
Conservative Protestants	41	30	29
Catholics	21	30	49
n of cases	1,336		
1980			
	Up to $11,999	$12,000 to $24,999	$25,000 and over
Liberal Protestants	24	36	40
Moderate Protestants	26	39	35
Conservative Protestants	32	36	32
Catholics	23	37	40
n of cases	621		

differences in the rates of increase among the four groups. Yet, once again, these differences were not particularly disadvantageous to the conservative Protestants. While they were slightly outpaced by the Catholics, overall the conservative Protestants were able to narrow the educational gap between themselves and the other major religious groups.[3]

Thus, on all three social measures the conservative Protestants were actually able to increase their relative social standing over the 20-year period from 1960 to 1980. For this reason there is every reason to doubt that the members of this group are currently suffering from a case of mass status threat due to a loss of social prestige. It seems evident that these particular definitions of status and status displacement are of little value to us in our attempt to explain the apparent recent increase in the political activity of the religious right.

For most students of religious-political change, however, this finding would probably be not at all surprising. A great deal of social science literature on the rise of the religious right in recent American politics is now beginning to emerge. In their attempt to explain this phenomenon many of these scholars are in one way or another making use of the concepts of status and status threat. However, the use of the status concept in this new body of literature seems to be more consistent with the second definition of status developed in Chapter 1. In this case status refers not to social prestige but to one's style of life. Status groups are defined by a common life-style and status threat occurs when the social changes taking place in society cause a particular status group to feel that the continuation of its style of life is somehow imperiled. It has been argued that the process of modernization in American society has produced a number of changes that are inconsistent with the style

TABLE 6.3
Religion by Education, 1960-80
(in percentages)

Denominational Category	Educational Category		
	Grade School	High School	College
1960			
Liberal Protestants	20	41	39
Moderate Protestants	26	49	26
Conservative Protestants	35	49	16
Catholics	24	61	15
n of cases	1,345		
1980			
Liberal Protestants	6	42	52
Moderate Protestants	7	50	43
Conservative Protestants	18	45	37
Catholics	8	49	43
n of cases	682		

of life that conservative Protestants tend to regard as the ideal. The recent upsurge in the political activity of the religious right can therefore be seen as an attempt to use government as an instrument for preserving or strengthening this ideal life-style.

What exactly is the style of life that conservative Protestant tradition holds to be ideal? While we would be unlikely to find universal agreement on all of the details, the central characteristics of this life-style are not difficult to discern. In its purest form, the conservative Protestant style of life flows directly from religious teachings. It is based on the belief that there is a right way and a wrong way to live, and that these can easily be determined from a knowledge of the Bible. Central to this life-style is the notion of the traditional family that is viewed as the basic unit of society. In the traditional family, each member is assigned specific roles—men as husbands, fathers, and breadwinners; women as wives and mothers—and these roles are not to be challenged. Children are to be raised strictly, thoroughly schooled in proper religious doctrine, and protected whenever possible from those temptations that could pull them off the path to salvation. Both inside and outside the family, life is seen as involving sets of clear-cut rules to be followed in order to attain heaven's reward. Religious belief is not viewed as simply one aspect of life but rather as its center or foundation and the ultimate source of meaning and order.

Thus explanations of the recent upsurge in the political activity of the religious right that emphasize life-style threat suggest that recent changes in American society have been perceived by conservative Protestants as being somehow threatening to this ideal style of life. This kind of explanation for recent religious-political events is quite consistent with the general model of such events that we derived from the historical material in Chapter 1. Yet in spite of its seeming plausibility this explanation is actually quite difficult to test. For this particular interpretation of events to be accurate, two things must be true. In the first place there must have occurred genuine social changes in recent years that could somehow be interpreted in a threatening manner by members of the religious right. In addition these objective events must have triggered subjective feelings of status or life-style threat among members of this particular religious group.

One only needs to take a brief look at the changes that have taken place in American society in the last 20 years to see that the first of these requirements has been fulfilled. The list of occurrences that one could expect to pose a threat to the conservative Protestant style of life includes such things as the banning of prayer in public schools, the legalization of abortion, the sexual revolution, the increase in the divorce rate, and the women's liberation movement. Many of these changes can be seen as especially threatening to the concept of the traditional family. The overwhelming rise in the percentage of marriages ending in divorce, the vast increase in both the occurrence and acceptance of illegitimate births, and the corresponding growth in the percentage of single-parent families constitute a direct threat to the traditional family structure. In addition the well-defined sex roles, which served to simplify the traditional life by narrowing its choices, have largely collapsed under the weight of ever-increasing percentages of women in the American work force. This has been accompanied by a new concern among women with career advancement as a means of achieving satisfaction in life.[4] To make matters worse, from the perspective of those who adhere to the conservative Protestant life-style, this same time period has seen the apparent denigration of much of traditional morality. This denigration has occurred especially, though not exclusively, in the realm of sexual behavior. In short, sex outside of the traditional marital context has come to be accepted by a large percentage of the population. Significantly, this fact is especially difficult to ignore since it is broadly reflected in movies, television, music, and other elements of mass culture. Even the legalization of abortion can be seen as yet more evidence of the separation of sexuality from the context of the traditional family.

Given these events, it would not be at all surprising to find greatly increased status anxiety among those people who adhere most closely to the traditional style of life that seems to be on the decline. However, it is not enough simply to assume such feelings. Rather we must look for ways to verify their existence in some empirical fashion. One possibility is to examine the content of the political appeals being made by organized groups on the religious right to see if they contain expressions of life-style threat. The following excerpt from a report issued by the Moral Majority of New York State just prior to the 1980 presidential election provides strong evidence for a life-style threat explanation of recent right-wing religious-political activity.

> The wicked naturally are the unsaved or ungodly, and certainly are in rule today in America. Why are the wicked in rule today?

Why do not the righteous reign? The answer, once again, is basic and simple. The wicked rule and oppress the righteous in our government today because of the irresponsibility of God's people in the political process. We, for the reasons of apathy and unconcern, have reaped the reaping and sowing rule in Galatians 6:7 that says, "Be not deceived; God is not mocked: for whatsoever a man soweth, that shall he also reap." Just as Lot reaped in Sodom and Gomorrah, so have we, because our salt became hard!

With a majority of the voting population in America either Christian or moral, America stands at the brink of God's judgment for her ungodly acts of national sin, and the Christians have the power to change her destiny.

Murder is legal, and millions of babies are killed every year. Drunkenness is the leading social problem in America. Narcotics, besides alcohol, are now legal. Gambling is now legal, along with open sex and pornography. Homosexuality and lesbianism [are] now being pushed as a normal way of life. The laws are not enforced. Satanism and Anti-Christ religions are everywhere. All prayer and Bible [have] been taken out of our schools! Why? The reason is the wicked beareth rule. We have left the destiny of our country to those who are unsaved and who are natural in mind.[5]

The basic sentiments expressed in this passage—the sense of loss of a style of life that was once dominant, and the need for political action to return the nation to this more righteous way of living—are consistent with the basic model of right-wing religious-political activity that was laid out in Chapter 1. Thus, evidence for a life-style threat explanation for the recent rise in the political activity of the religious right can be found in the movement's own political appeals. Still other evidence can be found in the movement's legislative agenda. Many of the goals of groups such as the Moral Majority have taken form in Congress with the introduction of the proposed legislation that has come to be known as the "Family Protection Act." Introduced by Senator Paul Laxalt, one of President Reagan's closest advisers, the bill includes provisions to:

- Prohibit subsidized public interest lawyers from handling cases involving desegregation or divorce.
- Explicitly legalize job discrimination against homosexuals.
- Require institutions receiving government funds to inform parents when their children request contraceptives or abortions.

- Deny federal education money to states that don't allow prayer in public buildings.
- Prohibit any federal attempt to outlaw spanking or tighten statutes against child abuse.[6]

These and other legislative goals of the modern religious right quite clearly express an attempt to strengthen the conservative Protestant style of life.

The evidence presented thus far seems to indicate the existence of life-style threat among organized groups on the modern religious right. But this does not necessarily mean that this type of status threat is widespread among the tens of millions of conservative Protestants who live in the United States. The right-wing activists who belong to groups such as the Moral Majority represent only a small portion of the conservative Protestant population. For this reason we need to find a way to measure the extent of life-style threat among this larger group of conservative Protestants. This is where the difficulty arises. Life-style threat is not a concept that easily lends itself to survey analysis. In addition, no national survey has yet been undertaken with this particular goal in mind. Nevertheless, some data are available in the form of a recent survey of the residents of the state of Florida.[7] Table 6.4 displays the responses of the members of each of the major religious groups to two questions from the survey that attempt to measure life-style threat. Specifically, the questions attempt to determine whether respondents find the social changes of the last 20 years to be inconsistent with what they regard as proper moral values. In many ways these changes would seem to represent a break with the traditional or orthodox Christian view of morality, which is a key underpinning of conservative Protestant teaching. Therefore, if these changes have indeed been culturally threatening, we would expect this to be especially true for the members of this particular religious group.

To some extent this expectation is borne out by the data in Table 6.4. The conservative Protestants are clearly more likely than members of the other religious groups to bemoan the moral changes that have taken place in American society in the last 20 years. However, it is also quite clear that this feeling that American society is on the moral downslide is quite widespread among all of the religious groups. This poses an interesting question. If large majorities of all the major religious groups seem to express concern

TABLE 6.4

Religion and Moral Decline, State of Florida, Nonblacks only (in percentages)

The personal moral values that I believe in have declined in American society in the last 20 years.

Responses: A. Strongly Agree
             B. Agree
             C. Not Sure
             D. Disagree
             E. Strongly Disagree

Denominational Category	*A*	*B*	*C*	*D*	*E*
Liberal Protestants	42	43	2	11	2
Moderate Protestants	44	39	6	11	1
Conservative Protestants	53	38	3	5	1
Catholics	37	49	4	8	2
n of cases	1844				

Because of changes in American society in the last 20 years, it has become more difficult for parents to instill proper moral values in their children.

Responses: Same as above.

Denominational Category	*A*	*B*	*C*	*D*	*E*
Liberal Protestants	31	47	5	15	2
Moderate Protestants	36	40	1	18	5
Conservative Protestants	46	37	1	14	2
Catholics	36	43	3	12	6
n of cases	1,853				

148

about the recent moral decline of American society, then why have groups such as the Moral Majority not had more success in affecting the political process?

In answering this question it is important to distinguish between those religious right activists who belong to groups such as the Moral Majority and the larger mass of conservative Protestants whom we have examined at many points in this book. The religious right activists can be viewed as a kind of elite group who constitute only a small portion of the 20 percent or so of the American electorate who happen to be conservative Protestants.[8] The evidence that we have seen does seem to indicate the existence of life-style threat among members of this elite group. As in similar periods in the past that saw heightened political activity among the religious right, this life-style threat should provide these elites with plenty of motivation to attempt to influence government policy. But to be successful they must be able to mobilize large numbers of ordinary voters behind their cause. Thus far this mobilization effort does not seem to have been as successful as similar efforts at other points in American history. For instance it in no way compares to the influence exerted by the religious right over the Republican party through the Ku Klux Klan in the 1920s.

There are many reasons to expect that the masses of conservative Protestants would be particularly responsive to the mobilization efforts of the new religious right activists. In the first place they are the most likely to share the religious beliefs of the religious right elites, including their strong orthodoxy and evangelistic bent. This means that they are the most likely to adhere to the elite's life-style as well. Therefore, we could expect the conservative Protestant masses to be more likely than the other religious groups to be threatened by recent changes in American society, an expectation that seems to be borne out by the findings of Table 6.4. Moreover, as discussed in Chapter 1, the theological tradition of the conservative Protestants makes them more likely than the other groups to favor using the powers of the state to achieve religious ends. Thus any attempt to understand the general lack of success of the new religious right activists should focus on their failure to mobilize the conservative Protestant masses. If they are unable to reach this group, it is not difficult to understand why they would have problems reaching the other religious groups as well.

So why have the Moral Majority and similar activist groups not been more successful at rallying the conservative Protestant masses to their cause? There are a number of possible explanations. For one thing, it may be that the bulk of conservative Protestants have not really been all that threatened by the apparent changes in American cultural values. The findings of Table 6.4 indicate that a large majority express concern about what they perceive to be a recent national moral decline. Yet it is far from clear whether this is indicative of a deeply felt life-style threat. In fact the overwhelming moral concern expressed by all of the religious groups in Table 6.4 may signal the existence of a certain ambivalence among many Americans regarding the direction in which American culture is moving. These figures seem to be somehow inconsistent with the rapid growth in such phenomena as drug usage, pornography, and premarital and extramarital sex. There appear to be an awful lot of Americans who express concern about moral decline while they at the same time participate in it. This contradiction may result from the different perspectives from which one can view recent cultural change. From a societal perspective this seeming breakdown in cultural norms can appear to be quite threatening. But from the individual perspective these same changes can offer a level of freedom that was unavailable to previous generations. The appeal of this new freedom is something that groups like the Moral Majority may have great difficulty in overcoming.

Thus it may be that the majority of conservative Protestants have not reached a level of life-style threat that would make them ripe for mobilization by the religious right elites. But another factor may be working to make the political efforts of the modern religious right activists less successful than similar efforts in the past. In his study of right-wing extremism in American history, Lipset identified an important element that added strength to the attempts by right-wing leaders to mobilize large portions of the mass population. This was the existence of a concrete population group that could be associated with the threat to the traditional style of life. The heavy Catholic and Jewish immigration of the nineteenth and early twentieth centuries provided right-wing leaders with convenient targets for their attacks;[9] but finding this sort of concrete target group has not been as easy for the modern religious right elites.

The latest threat to the conservative Protestant style of life seems to have resulted from the process of modernization and the emergence of what are often referred to as postindustrial values. However, it is difficult to attack a process, so a number of religious right leaders have sought to identify specific culprits that lie behind it. This has often led to attacks on so-called secular humanists who supposedly have worked their way into positions of influence and are leading the country down the path to destruction. In the words of Moral Majority leader Jerry Falwell, "A majority of secular humanists and amoralists are running this country and taking it straight to hell."[10] For the most part, however, these attempts to pinpoint blame have met with rather limited success. While in the past it was relatively easy to identify a Catholic or a Jew, it is difficult to determine exactly who or what a secular humanist is. Without such a clear-cut enemy it may be that religious right leaders will never be able to attain the level of influence of similar elites at various points in the past.

Finally the modern religious right elites have had the misfortune of having to compete with other, nonreligious concerns that have dominated the recent political agenda. Specifically the economic downturns of the 1980s have created severe economic hardships for many conservative Protestant voters. It should be remembered that in spite of the economic gains that they have made in recent decades, the conservative Protestants are still the poorest of the major American religious groups. Thus economic recessions are likely to hit hard, causing many of them to put aside cultural or life-style concerns and concentrate instead on bread and butter issues.

The relative failure thus far of modern religious right elites to mobilize conservative Protestant voters has acted to limit their influence within the political system. What are their prospects for the future? There are a number of possibilities. The efforts of the religious right elites could yet receive a boost from the further deterioration of traditional morality and the traditional family structure. At some point a threshold might be reached beyond which the perceived threat to their style of life might become great enough to cause a high percentage of conservative Protestants and smaller percentages of other religious groups to call for the kind of conservative social engineering advanced by such groups as the Moral Majority. However, it is more likely that the influence of the religious right elites will continue to be of a more limited nature. Depending on their political adroitness and willingness to compromise, these activists might succeed in transforming portions of their agenda into public policy by skillfully forming alliances with other types of conservatives. These efforts could be aided by an improving economy that could lessen the impact of bread and butter issues and increase the relative salience of life-style concerns. But the rigidity and religious zeal that has been demonstrated thus far by religious right leaders makes it just as likely that their movement will soon be relegated to the status of historical footnote. As is always the case when speculating about politics, only time will tell.

NOTES

1. One view, which has appeared in popular journals, is that the recent politicization of conservative religious groups is largely an outgrowth of larger organizational efforts being made by conservative political elites. According to these accounts it was actually these secular conservative organizers who took the original initiative in the founding of such religious groups as the Moral Majority. See "A Tide of Born-Again Politics," *Newsweek* 96 (September 15, 1980): 28-36.

2. It is interesting to note that much of the relative gain in income made by Catholics after World War II had already occurred by 1960. The more impressive gains made by Catholics after 1960 occurred in the educational realm.

3. In addition, recent work on elite religious right activists suggests that they tend to come disproportionately from high education and occupation brackets. This would seem to cast doubt on a social prestige explanation for the recent upswing in their political activity. See Clyde Wilcox, "The Ohio Moral Majority: A Case Study of the New Christian Right," a paper presented at The American Political Science Association Meeting, Chicago, September 1983.

4. A recent *New York Times* poll—conducted November 11-20, 1983— showed that American women were as likely to cite jobs as they were to cite being a wife and mother when asked what they found most satisfying about being a modern woman.

5. This statement was made by the chairman of the New York State Moral Majority. It is drawn from Dr. Dan C. Fore, "The Christian and Politics," *Moral Majority Report of New York State*, 1 (September 1980): 16.

6. "Religious Right Goes for Bigger Game," *U.S. News and World Report*, 89 (November 17, 1980): 42.

7. This survey was conducted by the Policy Sciences Center at Florida State University in January 1982. Though it is not a national survey, it is unlikely that any differences found between religious groups will be completely unique to the residents of Florida.

8. The Moral Majority is now thought to have 400,000 members nationwide rather than the millions that have sometimes been claimed. A recent study of the Ohio Moral Majority found that the membership lists contained only 285 names, not the 20,000 that the organization claimed. See Wilcox.

9. Seymour Martin Lipset and Earl Raab, *The Politics of Unreason: Right Wing Extremism in America, 1790-1977* (Chicago: University of Chicago Press, 1978).

10. Rev. Jerry Falwell, as reported in "Politics from the Pulpit," *Time* 116 (October 13, 1980): 35.

7

Religion and Party Identification

PARTY ATTACHMENTS AND GENERATIONAL CHANGE

Political scientists who study American electoral behavior have tended to distinguish between two different types of political forces that may affect the voting decision. Since the attitudes that individual voters hold toward the various candidates and issues of the day are likely to vary greatly from election to election, they are often referred to as short-term electoral forces. These highly volatile political attitudes are often contrasted with a more enduring electoral factor: the psychological identifications that many voters develop with one or another of the major political parties. In previous chapters we have been concerned mainly with the ways that religious beliefs can affect presidential voting behavior by first affecting the development of political attitudes. Since these attitudes are likely to undergo relatively rapid change, it could be expected that this sort of religion effect would vary considerably from election to election. But it is also possible for religion to exert a more enduring influence on the vote by affecting the formation of partisan identification. In Chapter 2 we uncovered evidence that in the years between 1960 and 1980 partisan identification did in fact seem to be amenable to this sort of religious influence. In this final chapter we would like to take a somewhat closer look at how this influence comes about.

154

The main concern of our research is, of course, presidential voting behavior. Then why should we be concerned with partisan identification? This question can be answered in two ways. In the first place partisan identification has been shown to exert a major influence on the presidential voting decision. Thus, in order to completely understand the vote we must determine the factors that cause individuals to identify with or fail to identify with a political party. In addition, understanding party identification tells us something about the future. Although party identification has been shown to be a relatively stable political force, it is not immune to change. The real significance of this change stems from its ability to affect future voting behavior. Therefore, by understanding the present we can gain insight into what is likely to happen in the future.

Since we are mainly concerned here with changes in partisan identification, it is imperative that we understand the process by which this change tends to come about. As stated above, although party identification tends to be more stable than actual presidential voting behavior, it is not immune to change. The same kinds of political events that affect the formation of short-term political attitudes may also, if they are salient enough, begin to affect the distribution of party identification in the electorate. With the exception of certain highly volatile electoral periods, this sort of partisan change is likely to be gradual in nature.[1] In addition, not all individuals are equally susceptible to such change. Research has shown that the strength of partisan identification in a given individual tends to increase over time. Therefore, in general young voters will be the most highly susceptible to partisan change.[2] For this reason it is important that we divide voters into different age categories. It is possible that relatively modest changes in the distribution of party identification in the electorate as a whole could mask much larger changes among the young.

In order to undertake our analysis we have broken down each of our four religious groups by party identification while controlling for age. The results of this process are displayed in Table 7.1.

Table 7.1 contains a great deal of information, but we are concerned here with uncovering only significant trends in the data. In Chapter 2 we were able to uncover partisan trends in the electorate as a whole, which seemed to be related to religious belief. Specifically, it was found that the well-documented dealignment

TABLE 7.1

Religion by Party Identification by Age, 1960-80

(in percentages)

Denominational Category	Year					
	1960	1964	1968	1972	1976	1980
Under 36						
Liberal Protestants						
Dem.	17	38	41	16	30	19
Ind.	18	19	30	52	42	44
Rep.	65	43	30	32	27	38
Moderate Protestants						
Dem.	55	37	27	24	20	28
Ind.	18	33	40	38	44	45
Rep.	27	30	33	38	36	28
Conservative Protestants						
Dem.	64	55	21	35	28	41
Ind.	28	17	50	36	45	27
Rep.	8	28	29	29	26	32
Catholics						
Dem.	72	55	46	46	43	36
Ind.	18	27	36	41	44	39
Rep.	11	18	18	12	14	25
n of cases	295	238	217	420	419	216
36 through 55						
Liberal Protestants						
Dem.	36	41	31	26	25	29
Ind.	26	14	34	29	34	31
Rep.	39	46	35	45	41	39
Moderate Protestants						
Dem.	26	48	31	31	32	33
Ind.	26	22	27	36	34	32
Rep.	49	30	42	33	34	35

Denominational Category	Year					
	1960	1964	1968	1972	1976	1980

36 through 55						
Conservative Protestants						
Dem.	62	76	59	51	37	38
Ind.	14	9	29	27	29	30
Rep.	24	15	12	23	34	32
Catholics						
Dem.	65	59	57	53	47	43
Ind.	22	25	25	28	31	31
Rep.	13	17	18	20	22	27
n of cases	541	392	366	455	415	230
56 and Over						
Liberal Protestants						
Dem.	32	40	34	31	21	30
Ind.	7	14	27	17	23	32
Rep.	61	46	40	52	55	38
Moderate Protestants						
Dem.	35	42	33	30	31	26
Ind.	21	11	17	19	27	34
Rep.	44	47	49	50	42	40
Conservative Protestants						
Dem.	64	74	54	51	58	61
Ind.	8	10	25	17	19	20
Rep.	29	17	21	32	23	20
Catholics						
Dem.	62	67	57	60	60	55
Ind.	21	11	20	17	20	28
Rep.	17	22	22	23	20	17
n of cases	344	249	240	373	425	235

Source: Compiled by the author.

of the electorate that began in the 1960s did not occur in the same manner among each of the religious groups. Among liberal Protestants the growth in the number of Independents between 1960 and 1980 occurred mainly at the expense of the Republicans. Among conservative Protestants, on the other hand, this partisan dealignment occurred primarily at the expense of the Democrats. In addition it was found that for both of these groups the critical period of change seemed to be the years from 1964 through 1972. All of these facts hinted strongly at the presence of powerful political forces that were somehow related to religious belief. The findings of Chapter 5 added credibility to this conclusion by suggesting that many of the new political issues of this period invoked attitudes that were influenced by religious belief. In Chapter 2 it was also shown that partisan dealignment among Catholics during the years from 1960 through 1980 occurred in a manner quite different from that of either of the Protestant groups, gradually developing over the entire 20-year period.

It remains for us to see if we can gain added insight into the above findings by controlling for age. If prior research in the field is correct, we can expect that the trends that we uncovered in Chapter 2 occurred unevenly among the various age cohorts. Specifically, these trends should have been much stronger among young voters than among their more senior counterparts. If this is the case it could have important implications regarding the future partisan makeup of the American electorate.

The findings of Table 7.1 do seem to bear out this general prediction.[3] Among liberal Protestants the decline in Republican strength and the growth in the number of Independents between 1960 and 1980 occurred most heavily among the youngest age category (although a surprising amount of change occurred among the oldest group as well). Among conservative Protestants losses among the Democrats and corresponding gains among the Independents and Republicans were concentrated in the two youngest age categories. Interestingly enough those in the youngest category were more likely than those in the middle category to move all the way into the Republican party, while those in the latter category tended to become Independents. (The growth in the Republican ranks among the middle age group in the 1970s was probably a result of the aging of those new voters who had identified with the Republican party in the 1960s.) Among Catholics the gradual growth in the percentage of Independents seemed to result from the failure of young voters to follow the lead of their elders and identify with the Democratic party (with the middle category slowly becoming more Independent as these younger voters aged over the course of the 20-year period).

What do these data imply about the future of American politics? All of the findings that we have presented seem to indicate that the years between 1964 and 1972 were ones in which religion played a major role in American electoral politics. During these years the national political agenda was dominated by issues that were in one way or another significantly related to religious belief. These issues came to play major roles in the outcomes of the presidential elections of 1968 and 1972. Of more importance for the long run, however, they also seem to have been salient enough to affect significantly the distribution of partisan identification in the electorate. By the late 1970s both parties had lost strength as the percentage of Independent voters soared. But the base of support that each party could rely on had changed in composition as well as in size. While the Democratic party had lost strength disproportionately among Catholics and conservative Protestants, its opposition had lost support mainly among the liberal Protestants.[4] Because these trends occurred disproportionately among the young, the possibility exists that their effects may be greatly magnified with the passage of time.

IMPLICATIONS FOR THE FUTURE

Looked at from the perspective of those who study party systems, these findings would seem to represent yet more evidence that the party coalitions formed during the New Deal had begun to crack under the strain of the new cross-cutting issues of the 1960s. Arising out of the midst of the Great Depression, the New Deal party system was based largely on class-related issues. The Democratic party of Franklin Roosevelt did more than simply preside over the national economic recovery. It had dedicated itself to the principle that the federal government was a proper instrument for bringing about the redistribution of income from the higher to the lower economic classes. This principle found direct expression through a variety of programs aimed at creating jobs and guaranteeing a minimum income for large segments of the population. In addition, through its favorable treatment of organized labor, the newly revised Democratic party sought to create an environment that would enable the working classes to demand from their employers a larger share of the economic pie. It was rather obvious that such policies were not always in the interest of those who for one reason or another found themselves positioned closer to the top of the economic hierarchy.

Quite naturally the new Democratic coalition came to be centered around organized labor and those groups who had fared the worst under the economic policies of previous administrations. Just as naturally the Republican coalition centered around big business and the upper economic classes. In terms of religious denomination, the strengthening of the class factor enabled the Democratic party to reinforce its hold on the poorer religious groups, the Catholics and the conservative Protestants. The Republicans in turn drew disproportionately from the wealthier liberal Protestant group.

In spite of the success of the Eisenhower presidential campaigns, the basic New Deal alignments remained essentially intact until the 1960s. At this time new issues such as Vietnam, civil rights, and law and order came to dominate the political agenda. These new issues differed from New Deal issues in that they tended to divide the electorate along something other than class lines. As indicated earlier, the appeal of these issues seemed to be related to the divisions of religious belief inherent in American society. This new religious division contributed to the fracturing of the largely class-based party coalitions that had existed for three decades.

The most clear-cut indication of this breakdown was the sudden rise in the number of Independents beginning in the mid-1960s. As young voters came of age they were less likely to find meaning in the old class-based battles of the New Deal, which had tended to form the basis of their parents' party affiliations. It was the new issues that seemed of greater relevance to them at this very formative period in their political lives. Often this younger generation of voters found their issue concerns to be either unrelated to or inconsistent with the partisan attachments of their parents. In many cases this resulted in the failure of young voters to identify with either of the major political parties. As time went on the process of generational replacement led to a steady rise in the number of Independents in the electorate.

As we have seen, this partisan breakdown did not occur in the same manner among all of the religious groups. The weakening of the class factor and the rise of the new cross-cutting issues led to a rapid decline in Republican support among liberal Protestants and Democratic support among conservative Protestants. These differences in the direction of partisan dealignment were a logical outgrowth of the rise of the new religion-related issues, on which liberal Protestants were more likely to take liberal stands than their conservative Protestant counterparts. By the end of 1980 some of these trends had been reversed, with class seeming to reemerge as the major basis for partisan division.[5] In speculating about the future, however, certain things should be kept in mind. One is that the political events of the 1960s offer stark evidence that the American party system has become highly volatile in nature. It is now clear that new types of issues that call upon something other than class self-interest can find their way onto the national political agenda. Some of these issues have the capacity to cause voters to divide up along the lines of religious belief. Thus religion and economic class can be seen as competing factors that can determine the outcome of a given presidential contest. The importance of this stems from the fact that very different party coalitions are likely to result from an election based on religion than from one based on class. A liberal Protestant, for instance, may find himself drawn toward the Democratic party when religion-related issues dominate and to the Republican party when class-based issues are dominant. In each case conservative Protestants are more likely to be pulled in the opposite direction. In addition, this electoral volatility is enhanced by the fact that there are today many more Independents among all the religious groups than there were in the years before the mid-1960s. Thus at the beginning of any presidential campaign there are more voters who potentially could be swayed by either of the major political parties.

Where exactly do the Catholics fit into this overall picture? Throughout the years of the New Deal era Catholics formed a critically important part of the Democratic coalition. The long-standing hold of the Democratic party on American Catholics received substantial reinforcement from the policies of Franklin Roosevelt. The attempts made by the Roosevelt administration to bring down unemployment, establish a level of income security, and remove some of the roadblocks to union organizational efforts found a receptive audience among the largely working-class Catholic population that had been hard hit by the economic downturn of 1929. This Catholic support for the Democrats reached a peak when a Catholic, John F. Kennedy, received the party's nomination for president in 1960. This election contest, which witnessed an inordinate amount of attention being paid to Kennedy's religious affiliation, resulted in the mobilization of millions of Catholic voters behind the Democratic candidate.

However, the very popularity of the Kennedy presidency may have had the effect of actually weakening the Democratic hold on the Catholic population. The popular appeal of the young president, which took on mythical proportions after his tragic assassination in 1963, went a long way toward attaining for Catholics the kind of acceptance into American society that had previously eluded them. This new acceptance meant that in the future it would be easier for many Catholics to support a Republican party that had so often in the past acted as a vehicle for the nativist and anti-Catholic elements in the political system. But something else was happening that provided a potentially larger threat to the historic link between the Democratic party and Catholic voters. This was the substantial economic progress being made by Catholics in the postwar years. In the realm of income and later in the realm of education Catholics were making substantial gains relative to the other religious groups. Over time more and more Catholics found themselves on the other side of the class appeals being made by Democratic politicians. It is this changing class factor that probably best accounts for the steady erosion in the percentage of Catholics identifying with the Democratic party in the years between 1960 and 1980. Thus the entrance of new generations of Catholics—better-educated and economically more successful than their parents—into the political system has provided new opportunities for the Republicans to expand their base of support.

Yet it is far from clear whether the Republican party can take full advantage of these new opportunities resulting from the changing class factor. As we have seen, class-based issues are not the only kinds of issues that can affect the outcome of a presidential election. Religion-related issues can in any given election year come to the forefront. As Chapter 5 indicated, on religion-related issues Catholics tend to be relatively liberal. This was found to be true for social and economic issues such as civil rights, moral issues such as school prayer, and foreign policy issues such as Vietnam. To the extent that these types of issues dominate a presidential race, it could be difficult for a conservative-oriented Republican candidate to rally Catholic voters around himself and his party.

The events of recent years would seem to indicate that it is the foreign policy type of issue that could provide the biggest obstacle to any major Republican effort to rally Catholic voters behind their cause. There is now substantial evidence to suggest that major changes have occurred in the way that American Catholics view their role in the shaping of their nation's foreign policy. In the years following World War II, American Catholics tended to endorse wholeheartedly the general policy of containment that was followed by presidential administrations of both political parties. There were a number of reasons for Catholic support of this foreign policy scheme, designed to stop the spread of communism in all areas of the world. One reason had to do with the strong anticommunist stand taken by church officials in the Vatican. In America this position found a particularly receptive audience among the many Catholics who traced their roots to nations that had recently fallen under Soviet domination. In addition the immigrant status felt by most Catholics caused them to be reluctant to criticize their own government in its dealings with foreign powers. In the words of one prominent Catholic clergyman, "Being an immigrant church, we wanted to show we were more American than anyone."[6]

However, a number of events have acted together to radically alter the relationship between the Catholic population and the formation of American foreign policy. The gradual acceptance of Catholics into the larger society brought with it the kind of political security that allowed them to cast a more critical eye on the doings of the foreign policy establishment. Here again the election of John Kennedy as president can be seen as a major turning point. While this was happening other events were occurring that made it more likely that many Catholics would begin to find fault with certain aspects of their country's foreign policy. As the 1960s got under way a new pope, John XXIII, began to modify the Vatican stance on how best to deal with world communism. The Second Vatican Council muted the church's fierce anticommunism and began to place emphasis on achieving social justice and peace.[7] In America the tragic outcome of American military intervention in Vietnam resulted in a serious breakdown in the general bipartisan consensus that had dominated American foreign policymaking in the postwar years. Disillusionment with the Vietnam War led many Americans to begin to challenge the concept of the United States as a kind of world policeman, obligated to intervene in hot spots throughout the globe in order to prevent possible gains in communist influence. A second broad foreign policy view began to emerge, one that to one degree or another emphasized greater restraint in the use of American military power as a means of solving world problems. By the summer of 1972 this less-interventionist view of American foreign policy had begun to gain the upper hand in the Democratic party.

The breakdown of the general foreign policy consensus that had existed before Vietnam greatly increased the chances that foreign policy issues would play a major role in future presidential elections. As the foreign policy debate increases in intensity, it becomes ever more likely that religious beliefs will play an important role in affecting the attitudes of individual voters regarding this issue area. It is this issue area that may provide Republican strategists with their greatest problems as they attempt to draw Catholic voters into the Republican fold. While it may be getting easier for Republicans to lure Catholic voters with class-based appeals, it may be becoming increasingly difficult to appeal to them on foreign policy.

In Chapter 5 we discussed how the basic religious beliefs of American Catholics could lead them to take relatively liberal stands on foreign policy issues. Specifically, Catholic theology was seen as being less likely than conservative Protestant theology to cause its adherents to view the international arena as yet another aspect of the struggle between good and evil. The rejection of such notions could be expected to make Catholics more open to diplomacy and compromise as an alternative to the use of military force in dealing with our international adversaries. These predictions concerning the influence of religious belief on foreign policy attitudes seemed to be borne out by the issue data from 1972.

Thus there are elements in the religious belief systems of American Catholics that have the potential to lead them to adopt liberal attitudes on certain foreign policy issues. As we have seen, in the years before the Vietnam War there were many factors that led Catholic voters to accept unquestioningly the basic assumptions that underlay the policy of containment. But changes in their group status, together with the breakdown of the general bipartisan consensus on foreign policy, have led many Catholics to reevaluate previously held views. Much of this reevaluation has come among the generation that has reached voting age in the years since the mid-1960s. The result of all this has been the increasing possibility that Catholics will fall back on centrally held religious beliefs as they seek basic principles to guide them in the reformulation of their foreign policy views.

Evidence for the existence of this religious influence began to appear at least as early as 1972. As the debate over the Vietnam War intensified and spread from college campuses to the general population, Catholics became more likely than the other major Democratic group, the conservative Protestants, to favor a non-military solution. But other evidence of rising foreign policy liberalism among Catholics has appeared in more recent years. Numerous observers have reported on the important role that Catholic activists have come to play in movements that seek to oppose Reagan administration policies in central America and in the field of nuclear arms. On the issue of central America Catholic groups have been out front in criticizing a policy that they say puts too much emphasis on military action and not enough on human rights. But the most intense opposition to the Reagan administration among Catholic foreign policy activists has come on the issue of nuclear arms. Here criticism has centered around the Reagan arms buildup and the perception that his administration has not been serious about negotiating an end to the nuclear arms race. All in all this recent political activity in the Catholic community has created a major headache for the Republican party in general and the Reagan administration in particular. In the words of one prominent observer of Catholic life, "There has never been anything like this head-to-head confrontation between the church and U.S. foreign policy."[8]

Significantly this new Catholic activism in the foreign policy arena has involved both laity and clergy. The easing of the Vatican's traditional hard-line stand against communism has led many in the American clergy to join the laity in reevaluating their foreign policy positions. Not surprisingly, these clergymen have also tended to rely heavily on religious belief in reformulating their policy stands. Recent foreign policy pronouncements by prominent clergy show evidence of the influence of that aspect of church doctrine that places emphasis on man-to-man ethics. In fact, it is the concern with human rights that is at the heart of objections to the Reagan administration's positions on both central America and nuclear arms. The most obvious example of this concern is the recent letter on nuclear policy that was adopted by an overwhelming margin of 238 to 9 by the American Catholic bishops. The letter, which calls for a halt in the spread of nuclear arms, questioned the morality of commonly accepted nuclear doctrines. The letter's wording suggests that such weapons are so inhumane that their use cannot be justified even to counteract an attack by conventional forces. "We do not perceive any situation in which the deliberate initiation of nuclear warfare on however restricted a scale can be morally justified."[9]

These sorts of liberal foreign policy pronouncements on the part of the church hierarchy can serve only to reinforce the liberal attitudes that have emerged in many of the Catholic laity. In the case of the bishops' letter, an enormous effort is being made to achieve just such an end. Over 1 million copies were quickly distributed and in many dioceses priests were urged to emphasize the letter in homilies and special services. "What we are really trying to do," said one bishop, "is to get our people to think in terms of peace rather than in terms of war."[10]

Thus there is strong evidence of rising foreign policy liberalism among Catholics, even as their economic successes move them in the conservative direction on class-based issues. The significance of both of these trends is heightened by the fact that they appear to be strongest among the young.[11] In this regard young Catholics have come to resemble their generational counterparts among the liberal Protestants. In any future party system based on class it is these two groups that could provide the bulk of Republican support.[12] On the other hand the relative liberalism of both groups on most religion-related issues could create problems for a party that has tended in recent years to adopt conservative positions on issues of this type. For the Democrats it would make great sense to take advantage of this incompatibility, especially in the area of foreign policy, since it will become increasingly difficult for them to win presidential elections if they do not do something to offset the erosion of Catholic support. Pitted against both Catholics and liberal Protestants are the conservative Protestants, whose religious beliefs tend to make them conservative on religion-related issues while their relative lack of wealth tends to make them liberal on issues based on class. Democrats can best woo them with class-based appeals, especially in times of economic hardship, while Republicans need to neutralize economic issues of this type and concentrate on playing to their religious conservatism.

From the perspective of strategists in both parties this sort of electoral volatility provides both great risks and opportunities. In a very real sense there is today no major party in America, at least when it comes to presidential elections. Majorities must be created anew in every successive election. This is where the skill comes in, for building a majority requires the ability to make the proper combinations of issue appeals to the right groups at any given point in time. The task seems even more difficult when we consider that most political leaders will to one extent or another wish to remain true to their own political philosophies and guiding principles. The solution may lie in the ability of a given leadership group to define issues in ways that will help their own causes. For instance it makes a great deal of difference whether a social program is seen as an attempt to steal from the hard-working middle class or a humanitarian effort to get the poor back on their feet. Thus the ability to define political issues may be more important than ever in this era of electoral instability. This ability is in turn dependent on an understanding of the basic values of individual voters. Those who succeed in understanding these values will find themselves in a better position not only to understand the past but to determine the future.

NOTES

1. A certain amount of fluctuation in the distribution of party identification in the electorate is likely to occur in response to the short-term forces at work in a given election. If the fallout from these political events extends over a period of elections it can lead to gradual systematic changes in the partisan distribution. This sort of change, which can have extremely important implications for future voting behavior, is often referred to as secular realignment. See V. O. Key, "Secular Realignment and the Party System," *Journal of Politics*, May 1959.

2. Evidence that partisan attachments grow stronger the longer a voter is identified with his party can be found in Philip E. Converse, "Of Time and Partisan Stability," *Comparative Political Studies 2* (July 1969): 139-67. In the American system this means that the strength of partisan identification is likely to increase with age, since the American party system in the twentieth century has been extremely stable relative to party systems in other countries.

3. It should be pointed out that these findings regarding the religious effect on the formation of party identification are meant to be merely suggestive. Since our main concern is voting behavior rather than party identification itself, no attempt has been made to implement controls for other social factors.

4. The implications of these partisan trends for future presidential voting behavior are, of course, heavily dependent on the reasons for their occurrence. The 1972 issue data are helpful here. The notion that young liberal Protestants were moving away from the Republican party because of their relatively liberal stands on religion-related issues is strongly supported by the

fact that young liberal Protestants were more liberal than their elders on each of the issues, and that among liberal Protestants under 36, Independents were more liberal than Republicans on each of these issues. The notion that young conservative Protestants were moving away from the Democratic party because of their relatively conservative stands on religion-related issues is supported by the fact that among conservative Protestants under 36, both Independents and Republicans were more conservative than Democrats on most issues. The findings for young Catholics are a bit more complicated. Their gradual movement away from the Democratic party seems inconsistent with their relatively liberal stands on religion-related issues. However, two things need to be mentioned. In the first place, prior to 1980 young Catholics gradually became more Independent but not more Republican. The 1972 data show that among this group Independents were actually more liberal than Democrats on a number of important religion-related issues. Thus, many young Catholics probably failed to identify with the Democratic party in spite of their liberal issue stands. This suggests that Democratic losses among young Catholics may not have been as significant as they seemed. In the second place, among the youngest Catholic group, Independents tended to be significantly more conservative than Democrats on the class-related issue of government job guarantees. This suggests that some of the Democratic losses among young Catholics may have been a result of class factors. Because of the gains in income and education made by Catholics relative to other religious groups in the last few decades, young Catholics may be less likely than their elders to see themselves as belonging to the lower classes.

5.   The voting data in Chapter 3 suggested that the 1980 election was not one in which religion-related issues played a major role. The findings of Table 7.1 indicate that there was some tendency in 1980 for young Protestants to revert back to old patterns of partisan identification. Among liberal Protestants the Republicans made significant gains while the Democrats suffered heavy losses. Among conservative Protestants the Democrats managed a significant relative gain. A strong relative Republican gain also occurred among Catholics. All of this suggests that class rather than religion may have been the dominant factor in the 1980 election.

6.   "Catholics Take to the Ramparts", *Time* 119 (April 19, 1982): 48. (The clergyman quoted is Father Cuchuloin Moriority, who runs San Francisco's archdioscesan Social Justice Commission.)

7.   Ibid.

8.   Ibid. (The quote is from *Commonweal* editor James O'Gara.)

9.   "The Bishops vs the Bomb," *Time* 121 (May 16, 1983): 65.

10.   "Roman Catholic Consciousness-Raising Against Nuclear Arms," *New York Times*, December 16, 1983, p. B1. (The bishop quoted is Daniel P. Reilly of the Diocese of Norwich, Connecticut.)

11.   The 1972 issue data show that Catholics under 36 appear to be more liberal than their elders on both foreign policy questions. On the question of guaranteed jobs, which is the closest thing we have to a class-based question, the most liberal Catholics are those over 55.

12.   Some evidence for the existence of greater class-based conservatism among young Catholics can be found in the 1972 data. As we move from the

oldest to the youngest age cohorts, Catholics become less liberal on the guaranteed jobs question relative to the other two religious groups. In Chapter 5 it was shown that this question seems to tap into a class-based as well as a religion-based effect. The rising class-based conservatism among young Catholics seems to be offsetting some of the religion effect on this question.

Appendix:
Denominational Coding Scheme

MICHIGAN SURVEYS

1. Liberal Protestants
   - 112 Congregational
   - 153 Unitarian or Universalist
   - 120 Methodist
   - 116 Episcopalian, Anglican, Church of England
   - 115 United Church of Christ

2. Moderate Protestants
   - 124 Disciples of Christ
   - 110 Presbyterian
   - 111 Lutheran
   - 123 Baptist
   - 113 Evangelical and Reformed
   - 125 "Christian"

3. Conservative Protestants
   - 141 Missouri Synod Lutheran
   - 140 Southern Baptist
   - 138 Primitive Baptist or Free Will Baptist
   - 149 Other Fundamentalist
   - 152 Latter Day Saints, Mormons
   - 131 Church of God
   - 136 Church of Christ
   - 132 Nazarene or Free Methodist
   - 135 Pentecostal or Assembly of God
   - 126 Mennonite, "Amish"
   - 137 Salvation Army
   - 139 Seventh Day Adventist
   - 154 Jehovah's Witnesses

4. Catholics
   - 200 Roman Catholic
   - 700 Greek Rite Catholic

5. Jews
   - 300 Jewish

6. Eastern Orthodox
   - 710 Greek Orthodox
   - 711 Russian Orthodox
   - 712 Roumanian Orthodox
   - 713 Serbian Orthodox
   - 719 Other Orthodox

7. Non-Judeo-Christians
   - 720 Mohammedan
   - 721 Buddhists
   - 722 Hindu
   - 729 Other Non-Judeo-Christian Religions
   - 790 Other Religions

8. No Stated Preference
   - 728 Agnostics, Atheists
   - 998 None, DK, No Preference
   - 0000 Had no preference
   - 999 NA

9. Unclassified Protestants
   - 100 Protestant, No Denomination
   - 101 Nondenominational Protestant Church
   - 102 Community Church (no denomination)
   - 109 Other Protestant
   Unclassifiable Protestant Denominations

170

GALLUP SURVEY

1. Liberal Protestants
   - 171 United Church of Christ, Congregationalist, E and R
   - 151 United Methodist Church
   - 152 A.M.E. Zion Church
   - 153 A.M.E. Church
   - 154 Other Methodist
   - 155 Methodist
   - 131 Episcopalian

2. Moderate Protestants
   - 172 Christian Church (Disciples of Christ)
   - 161 Presbyterian Church in the U.S.
   - 162 United Presbyterian Church in the U.S.A.
   - 163 Other Presbyterian
   - 164 Presbyterian
   - 122 American Baptist Churches
   - 141 American Lutheran Church
   - 142 Lutheran Church in America
   - 144 Other Lutheran
   - 145 Lutheran
   - 126 Baptist
   - 123 The National Baptist Convention of America
   - 124 The National Baptist Convention, U.S.A., Inc.

3. Conservative Protestants
   - 121 Southern Baptist Convention
   - 125 Other Baptist
   - 112 Latter-Day Saints
   - 143 Missouri Synod Lutheran

4. Catholics
   - 200 Roman Catholic

5. Jews
   - 300 Jewish

6. Eastern Orthodox
   - 400 Orthodox

7. Non-Judeo-Christian
   - 581 Other Religion
   - 500 Other

8. None
   - 600 None

9. Unclassified Protestants
   - 173 Other Protestant
   - 174 Protestant Unspecified
   - 100 Protestant
   - 181 Other Religion (Protestant)

Bibliography

Campbell, Angus, Philip E. Converse, Warren E. Miller, and Donald E. Stokes. *The American Voter*. New York: John Wiley, 1960.

Converse, Philip E. "Of Time and Partisan Stability." *Comparative Political Studies* 2 (1969): 139-167.

——. "The Nature of Belief Systems in Mass Publics." In David Apter, *Ideology and Discontent*. New York: The Free Press, 1964.

Converse, Philip E., Warren E. Miller, Jerrald G. Rusk, and Arthur C. Wolfe. "Continuity and Change in American Politics: Parties and Issues in the 1968 Election." *American Political Science Review* 63 (December 1969): 1083-1105.

Gallup, George. "Religion at Home and Abroad." *Public Opinion* 2 (March-May 1979): 38-39.

Gusfield, Joseph. "Social Structure and Moral Reform: A Study of the Women's Christian Temperance Union." *American Journal of Sociology* 61 (November 1955): 221-232.

Jensen, Richard. *The Winning of the Midwest: Social and Political Conflict, 1888-1896*. Chicago: University of Chicago Press, 1971.

Key, V. O. "Secular Realignment and the Party System." *Journal of Politics* 21 (May 1959): 198-210.

Kleppner, Paul. *The Cross of Culture: A Social Analysis of Midwestern Politics, 1850-1900*. New York: The Free Press, 1970.

Latourette, Kenneth Scott. *A History of Christianity*. New York: Harper and Row, 1953.

Lipset, Seymour Martin. *Revolution and Counterrevolution: Change and Persistence in Social Structures*. New York: Doubleday, 1970.

Lipset, Seymour Martin, and Earl Raab. *The Politics of Unreason: Right Wing Extremism in America, 1790-1977*. Chicago: University of Chicago Press, 1978.

Miller, Arthur. "Partisanship Reinstated? A Comparison of the 1972 and 1976 U.S. Presidential Elections." *British Journal of Political Science* 8 (April 1978): 129-153.

Miller, Arthur H., Warren E. Miller, Alden S. Raine, and Thad A. Brown. "A Majority Party in Disarray: Policy Polarization in the 1972 Election." *American Political Science Review* 70 (September 1976): 753-778.

Miller, Warren E., and Teresa E. Levitin. *Leadership and Change: Presidential Elections from 1952 to 1976*. Cambridge, Mass.: Winthrop, 1976.

Miller, Warren, and Arthur Miller. "Issues, Candidates, and Partisan Divisions in the 1972 Presidential Election." *British Journal of Political Science* 5 (October 1975): 394-434.

Nie, Norman H., Sydney Verba, and John R. Petrocik. *The Changing American Voter*. Cambridge, Mass.: Harvard University Press, 1979.

Page, Ann, and Donald Clelland. "The Kanawha County Textbook Controversy: A Study of the Politics of Life Style Concern." *Social Forces* 57 (September 1978): 265-281.

Roof, Wade Clark. "Socioeconomic Differentials Among White Socioreligious Groups in the United States." *Social Forces* 58 (1979): 280-289.

Stark, Rodney, and Charles Y. Glock. *American Piety: The Nature of Religious Commitment*. Berkeley: University of California Press, 1968.

Sundquist, James L. *Dynamics of the Party System: Alignment and Realignment of Political Parties in the United States*. Washington, D.C.: The Brookings Institution, 1973.

Tawney, R. H. *Religion and the Rise of Capitalism: A Historical Study*. Gloucester, Mass.: Harcourt, Brace and World, 1962 (originally 1926).

Weber, Max. *The Protestant Ethic and the Spirit of Capitalism*. New York: Charles Scribner's Sons, 1958 (originally 1904-05).

Index